Hiking
Great Basin
National Park

by
Bruce Grubbs

FALCON®

HELENA, MONTANA

*A*FALCONGUIDE ®

Falcon® Publishing is continually expanding its list of recreation guidebooks. All books include detailed descriptions, accurate maps, and all the information necessary for enjoyable trips. You can order extra copies of this book and get information and prices for other Falcon guidebooks by writing Falcon, P.O. Box 1718, Helena, MT 59624 or calling toll free 1-800-582-2665. Also, please ask for a free copy of our current catalog. Visit our web site at http://www.falconguide.com

All photos by author.
Cover photo by Tom Gamache for Wandering Around Outdoors.

Library of Congress Cataloging-in-Publication Data
  Grubbs, Bruce (Bruce O.)
      Hiking Great Basin National Park / by Bruce Grubbs.
          p. cm.
      Includes bibliographical references and index.
      ISBN 1-56044-595-5 (pbk)
        1. Hiking—Nevada—Great Basin National Park—Guidebooks.
    2. Hiking—Nevada—Guidebooks. 3. Great Basin National Park (Nev.)-
  —Guidebooks. 4. Nevada—Guidebooks. I. Title.
  GV199.42.N32G744 1998
  917.93'15—dc21   97-46433
                                            CIP

♻ Text pages printed on recycled paper.

CAUTION

Outdoor recreational activities are by their very nature potentially hazardous. All participants in such activities must assume the responsibility for their own actions and safety. The information contained in this guidebook cannot replace sound judgment and good decision-making skills, which help reduce risk exposure, nor does the scope of this book allow for disclosure of all the potential hazards and risks involved in such activities.

Learn as much as possible about the outdoor recreational activities in which you participate, prepare for the unexpected, and be cautious. The reward will be a safer and more enjoyable experience.

Contents

Overview Map

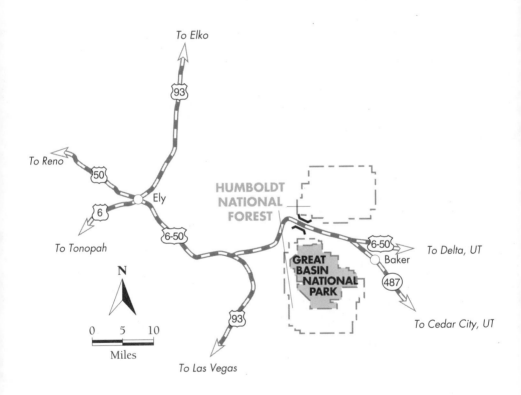

Map Legend

Interstate	(00)	Campground	▲
US Highway	(00)	Cabins/Buildings	■
State or Other Principal Road	(00) (000)	Peak	9,782 ft.
National Park Route	(00)	Hill	
Interstate Highway	⟹	Elevation	9,782 ft. ✕
Paved Road	⟹	Gate	•—•
Gravel Road	⟹	Overlook/Point of Interest	◘
Unimproved Road	==⟹	Pass/Saddle	) (
Trailhead	○	National Forest/Park Boundary	
Main Trail(s)/Route(s)			
Alternate/Secondary Trail(s)/Route(s)		Map Orientation	N
Parking Area	(P)	Scale	0 0.5 1
River/Creek			Miles
Lake			

Acknowledgments

This book would not have been possible without the help of many people and organizations. Thanks to Terry Baldino, Great Basin National Park, for providing a wealth of information and advice. I greatly appreciate the time Anne Hopkins and others at Great Basin National Park spent reviewing the manuscript. Thanks also to Janille Baker at the Great Basin Natural History Association for steering me through the existing literature and reviewing the manuscript. Thank you to the personnel at the Ely Ranger District, Humboldt National Forest, for reviewing the introductory material and the hikes in the Forest. Thanks to Jean Rukkila for proofreading and many valuable comments.

Special thanks to Jim Babbitt, Doug Rickard, and Duart Martin for accompanying me on trips to Great Basin National Park and the Snake Range, and putting up with my odd, photography-driven schedule. And finally, many thanks to my editor, Randall Green, and all the fine folks at Falcon Publishing for turning the manuscript into a finished book.

USGS Topographic Maps
Index

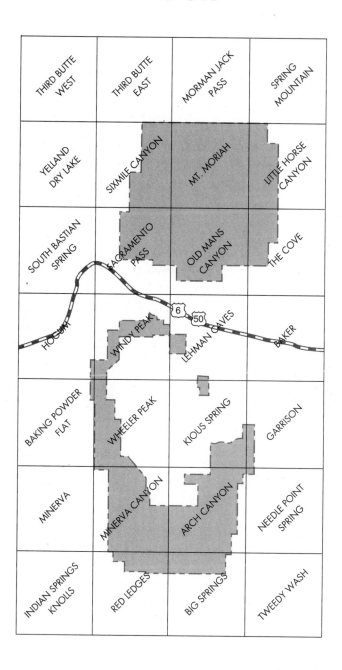

Jeff Davis Peak towers above the Wheeler cirque.

Introduction

The best-kept secret of Great Basin National Park is its incredible backcountry. If you like to visit stands of ancient trees as old as civilization, walk along a cascading mountain creek, camp in a cool mountain forest, or hike a high ridge with 100-mile views, then this is the region for you. And you don't have to be a "hiker" to enjoy it. As this book shows, there are hikes for beginners and non-hikers as well as experienced backpackers.

While this book focuses on Great Basin National Park, it also covers trails in the adjoining Humboldt National Forest and Mount Moriah Wilderness. These areas lie in the Snake Range along the eastern Nevada–central Utah border. The Snake Range is Nevada's second highest mountain chain, culminating in 13,063-foot (3,982-meter) Wheeler Peak. U.S. Highway 50 crosses the range at Sacramento Pass, dividing it into southern and northern sections. The southern Snake Range features Wheeler Peak and Great Basin National Park, and the northern Snake Range features the Mount Moriah Wilderness Area, crowned by its namesake peak, Mount Moriah, at 12,067 feet (3,678 meters).

Great Basin National Park was established in 1986 to preserve an outstanding section of the Great Basin. The park includes 77,100 acres (31,200 hectares) in the southern Snake Range. It also includes a remarkably diverse landscape, with desert sagebrush flats, piñon-juniper or pine-fir forests, subalpine forests, and alpine tundra. Lehman Cave, famous for its beautiful formations, is another attraction. Great Basin National Park features several well-maintained and primitive trails that lead to a natural arch, several alpine lakes, ancient bristlecone pine forests, and the top of Wheeler Peak. The remainder of the southern Snake Range is part of the Humboldt National Forest.

Mount Moriah Wilderness Area covers 82,000 acres (33,190 hectares) in the northern Snake Range. A unique feature of this wilderness is The Table, an 11,000-foot (3,350-meter) alpine plateau. The area offers an opportunity for solitude on infrequently traveled and minimally maintained trails.

One of my purposes in writing this book is to encourage visitors to stay at Great Basin National Park for an extended period. A tour of Lehman Cave and a drive up Wheeler Peak Scenic Road, though certainly worthwhile, barely scratch the surface of this diverse area. By hiking and exploring the backcountry of the park and the Snake Range, you will fully experience these wonderful mountains.

A good way to start your visit is at the visitor center. Permits are not currently required for day hiking or backpacking within the park, but it's a good idea to check with park rangers about water sources and backcountry trail conditions. The park encourages backcountry users to register for safety reasons. The visitor center has maps and books, as well as an informative display about the area. It is also the place to schedule a tour of Lehman Cave.

WEATHER AND CLIMATE

The Snake Range has a great variety of weather, partly because of its wide elevation range and partly because of its interior continental location. In the high country, summer and autumn are the best hiking seasons. The lower desert areas are most enjoyable in spring and fall. In winter and spring, significant amounts of snow usually blanket the high country, and the peaks become the domain of experienced winter mountaineers and backcountry skiers. Elevations in the park range from 6,200 feet (1,890 meters) to 13,063 feet (3,982 meters).

During summer, the valleys commonly reach temperatures of 90 degrees Fahrenheit (32 degrees Celsius) during the afternoon, and occasionally reach 100 degrees F (38 degrees C). Nights on the desert can be chilly, with temperatures dropping to 50 degrees F (10 degrees C) or lower. The high country is the place to be in summer, with high temperatures around 75 degrees F (24 degrees C). Nights in the mountains can be cold, even in summer, with temperatures dropping near freezing. In the fall, daily high temperatures in the desert drop to an average of 75 degrees F (24 degrees C). Winter temperatures in the mountains can drop as low as -30 degrees F (-34 degrees C), and occasionally reach subzero levels in the valleys as well.

The desert valleys and foothills receive about 10 inches (25 centimeters) of precipitation a year; the mountain crest may receive two or three times that amount. During summer, most of the moisture comes as rain from sporadic thunderstorms. By late October, the weather shifts to a winter pattern, and Pacific weather systems begin to reach the area. These storms bring snow to the mountains and rain to the valleys at first, but as winter approaches snow falls in the valleys as well.

Winter storms dominate the weather through April. Deep snow usually lingers into May on the peaks, but the foothills and lower canyons are often in prime condition for hiking in early season. Strong winds sometimes blow on the exposed ridges, and even during otherwise calm weather, the sharp temperature contrast at different elevations can cause strong upslope or downslope winds. This effect is especially noticeable in canyons and valleys.

The stormy periods are interspersed with stretches of fine weather. Even in December and January more than half the days are either clear or partly cloudy. During summer and fall cloudy days are an uncommon treat. As in most mountain areas, the weather can change rapidly; snow falls every month of the year on the peaks and ridges, and thunderstorms in particular can build up quickly.

Hendrys Creek.

Summit Trail to Wheeler Peak, with Mt. Moriah on the horizon.

WHAT IS THE GREAT BASIN?

Geographer I. C. Russell wrote an elegant description of the Great Basin in 1885:

> In the crossing from the Atlantic to the Pacific, between the Mexican boundary and the central portion of Oregon, one finds a region, bounded by the Sierra Nevada on the west and the Rocky Mountain system on the east, that stands in marked contrast in nearly all its scenic features with the remaining portions of the United States. The traveler in this region is no longer surrounded by the open, grassy parks and heavily timbered mountains of the Pacific slope, or by the rounded and flowing outlines of the forest-crowned Appalachians, and the scenery suggests naught of the boundless plains east of the Rocky Mountains or of the rich savannas of the Gulf States. He must compare it rather to the parched and desert areas of Arabia and the shores of the Dead Sea and the Caspian.
>
> The bare mountains reveal their structures almost at a glance, and show distinctly the many varying tints of their naked rocks. Their richness of color is sometimes marvelous, especially when they are composed of the purple trachytes, the deep-colored rhyolites, and the many-hued volcanic tuffs so common in western Nevada. Not infrequently a range of volcanic mountains will exhibit as many brilliant tints as are assumed by the New England hills in autumn. On the desert valleys the scenery is monotonous in the extreme, yet has a desolate grandeur of its own, and at times, especially at sunrise and at sunset, great richness of color. At midday in summer the heat becomes intense, and the mirage gives strange delusive shapes to the landscape, and offers false promises of water and shade where the experienced traveler knows there is nothing but the glaring plain. When the sun is high in the cloudless heavens and one is far out in the desert at a distance from rocks and trees, there is a lack of shadow and an absence of relief in the landscape that makes the distance deceptive—the mountains appearing near at hand instead of leagues away—and cause one to fancy that there is no single source of light, but that the distant ranges and the desert surfaces are self-luminous. The glare of the noonday sun conceals rather than reveals the grandeur of this rugged land, but in the early morning and near sunset the slanting light brings out mountain range after mountain range in bold relief, and reveals a world of sublimity. As the sun sinks behind the western peaks and the shades of evening grow deeper and deeper on the mountains, every ravine and cañon becomes a fathomless abyss of purple haze, surrounding the bases of gorgeous towers and battlements that seem encrusted with a mosaic more brilliant and intricate than the work of Venetian artists. As the light fades and the twilight deepens, the mountains lose their detail and become sharply outlined silhouettes, drawn in the deepest and richest purpose against a brilliant sky. (Harlan D. Unrau, *Basin and Range: A History of Great Basin National Park*)

This region of unique topography covers about 200,000 square miles (500,000 square kilometers) and includes nearly all of Nevada, much of western Utah, and parts of California, Oregon, and Wyoming. Within this vast area, some 160 mountain ranges, all trending north-south, separate more than 90 valley basins. The term Great Basin refers to the fact that all of the drainage from the mountains flows into interior basins and none reaches the sea. A few of these basins include permanent lakes, and some have seasonal lakes, but the majority of the valleys are dry. The mountain ranges tend to be long and narrow, from 30 to 120 miles long and 3 to 15 miles wide. Most ranges have peaks above 9,000 feet, and a dozen or so reach above 10,000 feet. The highest point is Boundary Peak, 13,140 feet (4,005 meters), located in the White Mountains near the California border. Although the Great Basin is a desert, the higher mountains catch enough moisture from passing storms to support forests, streams, and lakes.

HISTORY OF THE SNAKE RANGE

Prehistory

There is evidence that humans have occupied the Snake Range since about 9,000 to 12,000 B.C. These earliest people appear to have been small, mobile groups that spent their time gathering or hunting big game animals, including mammoths, bison, camels, ground-sloths, and horses.

Around 9,000 B.C., as the climate dried out, these native peoples began to use a wider range of plant and animal products as food sources and for clothing and implements. Evidence survives in the form of manos and milling stones, baskets, moccasins, spears, and digging sticks. Some artifacts show that these people traded with coastal California. By 500 B.C., people who lived in and near the Snake Range had settled into a distinctive lifestyle, living part of the year in small villages and supplementing their diet with hunting and food gathering. These people developed a characteristic artistic style, expressed in their pottery and rock art.

At the time of first European contact, the Native American group occupying the area was known as the Western Shoshone. They lived in small villages near water sources, occupying small, conical brush houses. During spring and summer, families dispersed to gather plant seeds and roots, and to hunt. In fall, the families held communal rabbit and antelope drives, and gathered piñon nuts. By winter, groups of families would congregate in small villages in the piñon-juniper zone, along the lower slopes of the mountains.

Explorers, Traders, and Trappers

Extensive European exploration of North America began with the voyage of Christopher Columbus in 1492. Two hundred and fifty years later the Great Basin still lay uncharted and unknown. By the 1770s, Spain had established missions in California and New Mexico, and was looking for an overland route to connect them. In 1776, the Garcés expedition explored the southern edge of the Great Basin, and the Escalante expedition reached a point about 80 miles east of the Snake Range.

The next explorations of the Great Basin were done by British and American fur trappers such as Peter Skene Ogden and Jedediah Smith. Ogden was the first to explore the northern Great Basin, discovering the Humboldt River in 1829, which would later become the route of the Overland Trail. Smith was the first to cross Sacramento Pass in the Snake Range in 1827.

Stella Lake.

Driven by desire for profits in the lucrative fur trade and competition between British and American interests in western North America, other trappers rapidly completed the exploration of the Great Basin by 1830.

John Charles Frémont led several early expeditions to explore and map the west, and in 1844 discovered that the huge region between the Sierra Nevada and the Wasatch Mountains did not drain to the sea. He was the first to use the term "Great Basin" to describe the area. After Mormon pioneers successfully settled the Salt Lake Valley in Utah, other members of the Church of Jesus Christ of Latter Day Saints began to spread over a much wider region. Some of their outposts survived, others failed. In 1855, the White Mountain Mission expedition attempted to establish a settlement at present-day Garrison on the eastern slopes of the Snake Range. Snake Creek Farm, as it was called, lasted only three years. Meanwhile, the ongoing expedition produced the first written record of exploration in Great Basin National Park, and was the first party to climb Wheeler Peak, known then as Jeff Davis Peak.

Emigrant Trails

With the establishment of the Old Spanish Trail through the southern Great Basin, and the Overland Trail across the northern Great Basin, emigrants bound for California started to traverse the inhospitable desert. The trickle of parties in the early 1830s became a flood by 1850, spurred on by discovery of gold in California in 1849. By then, the United States spanned the continent from coast to coast, and the government became interested in discovering practical routes across the Great Basin.

In 1855, Howard R. Egan explored a route that crossed the northern end of the Snake Range. Captain James H. Simpson of the U.S. Army was sent to the Great Basin in 1858 to reconnoiter a more direct route to California, and locate a site for a fort midway across the route. The Simpson expedition was the first scientific exploration to cross the Great Basin, and included a geologist, naturalist, photographer, and artist.

From 1859 to 1861, overland mail, stage, and telegraph services were begun along the Simpson–Egan route. The Pony Express was an ambitious express mail service on this route, one that was quickly outmoded by the completion of the transcontinental telegraph. Further changes took place when the transcontinental railroad was completed along the Humboldt River in 1869, and most freight and passenger traffic moved to the swifter railroad.

Government and Private Surveys

After the turmoil of the American Civil War ended, the federal government sponsored a series of scientific surveys in the Great Basin. In 1869, George M. Wheeler was made the leader of a reconnaissance survey of southern and southeastern Nevada, including the Snake Range. He and several of his men climbed the highest point in the Snake Range, which his men named Wheeler Peak in his honor. His report described in detail the forests, wildlife, and mining in the area, as well as the Native Americans.

John Muir, the famous naturalist and conservationist, visited the Snake Range in the late 1870s in the course of his survey of the resources of Nevada's mountain ranges. He climbed Wheeler Peak and noted the evidence of glacial activity there. His journals and notebooks became the basis of his later articles and books calling for the protection of America's natural resources.

In 1878, a new federal agency, the U.S. Coast and Geodetic Survey, was given the task of completing precise survey measurements across the country. The Survey established triangulation stations on many of the Great Basin's highest summits. Using a transit-like instrument called a theodolite, the surveyors were able to take accurate position measurements, which made it possible to survey the land for legal boundaries and produce reliable maps. Wheeler Peak was occupied for several seasons as part of this survey, and evidence of the survey station is still visible there.

Miners and Loggers

Discovery of the Comstock Lode in 1859 in western Nevada set off the first mining rush in the Great Basin. When the Comstock mines suffered a temporary depression in 1864, prospectors fanned out across the rest of Nevada. Discoveries were soon made in the Snake Range, but making a profit from ore was difficult in such remote country. Miners left their mark in every part of the range, in the form of prospect holes and small shafts, but few sites were ever developed into large mines. Among the more notable operations in the southern Snake Range were the Minerva tungsten mines, the Mount Washington copper-lead-antimony mines, the St. Lawrence lead-silver mine on the southwest slopes, the Osceola placer gold mine on the northwest slopes, and the Johnson tungsten mine on the crest at Johnson Lake.

Logging has never been a major industry in the Snake Range because of the range's small forested area. In the past, timber was cut mainly to satisfy the needs of the mines and settlers. At one time there were lumber mills in South Fork Big Wash in the south Snake Range and Hendrys Creek in the Mount Moriah area, among other sites.

Settlement

The area's population jumped during the mining boom and led directly to more permanent settlements. By 1869 a number of ranches and small farms had been established in Spring Valley and in Snake Valley, flanking the Snake Range. The settlers were dependent upon creeks flowing out of the mountains for their water supply, and on timber growing on the upper slopes for wood.

Well-known as the discoverer of Lehman Cave, Absalom S. Lehman established a ranch on a creek near the east boundary of the present-day Great Basin National Park in 1870. He discovered the cave in 1885, and exploration soon revealed its beautiful and extensive natural decoration. He began to advertise the cave and serve as a guide, and by 1887 was establishing a new ranch at the cave to serve as a tourist center. He sold his old ranch on Lehman Creek in 1891, but died before he could develop his new holdings.

The settlement of Baker was established by Ben Lehman (the brother of Absalom Lehman) and several others in the late 1870s. George W. Baker built a major cattle ranch at the town, which was later named for him. In 1911, the USDA Forest Service created a ranger station in Baker to administer the new Nevada National Forest, which included the Snake Range. Garrison was permanently settled about the same time as Baker by several families who began farming along lower Snake Creek.

The Snake and Spring valleys have always been difficult to reach by the standards of more populated regions. Railroad lines were extended to Ely, Nevada, and Milford, Utah, by 1906, which helped ranchers and miners transport products to market. U.S. Highway 50, the highway that crosses the Snake Range at Sacramento Pass, was completed by 1920 but not paved until 1947. Even today, the Snake Range is a long way from the nearest major cities.

Humboldt National Forest

By 1880, conservationists such as John Muir and others were advocating preservation of the country's forests and natural wonders. Because of their work, the first national parks were established by 1890. In 1891, national forest reserves were created, primarily to protect timber and watersheds. The Forest Service was created in 1905 under the Department of Agriculture to administer the forest reserves, which were redesignated national forests in 1907.

The present multiple-use and conservation policies of the Forest Service were largely developed by energetic Gifford Pinchot, the first chief forester. The Snake Range, including the future Great Basin National Park, was included in the Nevada National Forest, created by President Theodore Roosevelt, in 1909. As part of a major reorganization of the national forests, the Nevada National Forest was eliminated in 1957, and the Snake Range became part of the Humboldt National Forest.

Great Basin National Park

Cada C. Boak, a Tonopah mining broker and advocate of US 50, led the effort to create a national monument at Lehman Cave, starting in 1920. Two years later, President Warren Harding proclaimed Lehman Cave National Monument under the authority of the American Antiquities Act. The new monument was administered by the Forest Service until 1933, when Lehman Cave and all other national monuments were transferred to the National Park Service under the Department of the Interior in 1933. In deference to grazing and mining interests, just one square mile was protected in the national monument.

Shortly after the creation of the national monument, Boak and others began to advocate the idea of a national park in the Snake Range, but nothing came of these efforts. Interest revived in 1955, primarily due to the efforts of Weldon F. Heald, who became interested in the Snake Range after his rediscovery of Wheeler Glacier on a five-day hiking trip. Partly because of increasing public interest in preserving the southern Snake Range as a scenic and recreational area, the Forest Service designated the Wheeler Peak Scenic Area in 1959. As part of efforts to provide easy recreational access to the mountains, the Forest Service built the Wheeler Peak Scenic Road and constructed several campgrounds in the mid-1960s.

Over the years, several bills were introduced into Congress to create a Great Basin National Park, but none passed. Strong opposition from ranching and mining interests was a major factor in the defeat of the park proposals. But by the mid-1980s, the movement to create a park revived. Mining and ranching were no longer primary economic forces, and tourism was increasing. There was strong interest in protecting Nevada's remaining roadless areas as part of the National Wilderness Preservation System, primarily by residents of the populous Reno and Las Vegas areas. This led to revived interest in a national park and much debate between local and national advocates and opponents as to the size and exact boundaries of the park. Finally, Congress passed a bill which President Ronald Reagan signed on October 27, 1986, creating the present 77,000-acre Great Basin National Park, Nevada's first national park.

The new national park inherited the facilities of the old Lehman Cave National Monument, including the small visitor center, plus nearby Forest

Service campgrounds, roads, and trails. As the new park became more well known and visitation increased, it became apparent that changes would have to be made in order to administer the area as a coherent national park. By 1992, a general management plan called for the construction of a new entrance road and visitor center, and relocation and closure of some existing roads. Hikers would benefit from new hiking trails that would connect existing trails to form an expanded park-wide trail system.

Mount Moriah Wilderness

The Mount Moriah Wilderness Area protects 82,000 acres in the northern Snake Range under the jurisdiction of the Forest Service and the Bureau of Land Management. The wilderness was created in 1989 as part of the Nevada Wilderness Act, which protected many roadless areas in the Toiyabe and Humboldt national forests. Prior to that time, the Jarbidge Wilderness was the only designated wilderness area in Nevada.

Interest in protecting roadless areas had begun within the Forest Service in the 1930s, primarily under the influence of Aldo Leopold. The agency designated some places as wilderness closed to motorized travel, but these areas were protected only by administrative order. Wilderness advocates worked hard to gain more permanent protection for roadless areas, and their efforts resulted in the National Wilderness Preservation System created by Congress in 1964. The Wilderness Act immediately designated most existing national forest wilderness areas part of the Wilderness System, but left a few to be administratively protected by the Forest Service as primitive areas.

In wilderness areas, humans are intended to be temporary visitors. Permanent structures and motorized and mechanized vehicles, including bicycles, are kept out in order to preserve the primitive nature of the area. Mount Moriah Wilderness, together with the remainder of the Humboldt National Forest in the Snake Range, is presently administered by the Ely Ranger District, headquartered in Ely, Nevada.

Wind blown, "krummholz" limber pine below Wheeler Peak.

BACK COUNTRY SKILLS AND SAFETY

With experience, operating in the backcountry becomes a welcome relief from the complex tangle of civilized living. Wilderness decisions, though usually important, are also basic in nature. While "out there," hikers discover that what seemed important in civilization loses some of its urgency. In other words, we gain perspective.

Wilderness can be a safe place if you are willing to respect your limitations. Many backcountry accidents are caused by individuals or parties pushing too hard. Start with easy hikes and progress to more difficult adventures as your experience broadens and your equipment allows. Set reasonable goals, allowing for delays caused by weather, deteriorated trails, slow members of your party, unexpectedly rough country, and dry springs. Be flexible enough to eliminate part of a hike if your original plans turn out to be too ambitious. Do not fall into the trap of considering a trip plan cast in stone; instead, take pride in adaptability.

Day hiking is popular because it can be enjoyed over short periods of time. It also requires no specialized equipment; beginners often have all the gear needed. For many hikers, the step from day hiking to backpacking is a larger one. Somehow, the thought of sleeping out is daunting, as is the additional time, equipment, and skill required. However, the hiker who never stays out overnight is missing as much as the swimmer who only dangles his or her toes in the water. Start out easy by camping near a trailhead on a familiar trail, then gradually extend your range by camping farther from the road and staying out longer.

Good pieces of equipment, along with the skill and technique to use them, make hiking safer and more enjoyable. Experienced hikers with a modest amount of equipment also have less impact on the backcountry. On all hikes that are longer than a casual stroll, you should carry water, food, rain/wind gear, sunglasses, sunscreen, a knife, a lighter or other reliable fire starter, maps, a compass, and a flashlight. These items easily fit in a small fanny pack and may save your life if you are delayed or if the weather changes.

EQUIPMENT

Footwear

For short, easy hikes on good trails, nearly any comfortable footwear such as tennis shoes or running shoes will work. It is important that the shoe or boot fit snugly with plenty of toe room. Double-check children's hiking shoes, since kids are often unable to determine the proper fit for themselves and will not complain until it is too late. If you become an avid hiker, you may want to buy a pair of lightweight hiking boots. These are suitable for longer, rougher trails. There are many models available in women's, men's, and children's sizes, constructed of nylon with leather reinforcing and molded rubber soles. Some of the more sophisticated and expensive designs use waterproof/breathable fabrics. For difficult hiking with heavy loads, some hikers prefer leather boots with soles that can be replaced when they wear out. Others (including me) prefer lightweight boots even for difficult cross-country hiking.

High quality, well-fitting socks are critical to hiking comfort. They provide both insulation and padding. A good combination is a light inner sock of cotton, wool, or polypropylene, with an outer mid- to heavy-weight sock of wool with nylon reinforcing. The outer sock will tend to slide on the inner sock rather than directly on your skin, reducing the chance of blisters. Inner socks of cotton are comfortable in warm weather, and polypropylene socks will wick moisture away from your skin in cool weather. Wool is still the best fiber for the outer, cushioning sock, though small percentages of nylon and elastic materials help make the sock more durable.

Blisters should be treated **before** they happen! At the first sign of a hot spot or other discomfort on one of your feet, stop and have a look. A hot spot can be protected with a piece of felt or moleskin. Often a change of socks will help as well. Once a blister has fully developed, it should be protected by a piece of moleskin with the center cut out around the raised area of skin, like a donut. A large or deep blister can be immobilizing, which is why prevention is so important.

Clothing

Nearly any durable clothing will do for hiking in good, stable weather. On hot, sunny days, keep your skin covered with long sleeves and long pants, or use a good sunscreen. In the mountains, strong sun and high altitudes can produce painful sunburn in a short time, even on tanned skin. A brimmed sun hat is a good idea. Long pants will protect your skin from scratches when hiking a brushy trail.

Give a little more thought to your clothing in cool, windy, or changeable weather. Wearing several layers of light, flexible clothing works better than a single heavy, cumbersome layer such as a winter parka. In cool weather, a warm wool or synthetic fiber watch cap or balaclava makes an amazing difference in comfort—up to half your body's heat is lost through your head. Protect your hands with wool or synthetic gloves or mittens.

The layer system becomes even more important when you are backpacking, because you'll want to keep your load as light as possible. A four-layer system can handle nearly any weather condition. The first, inner layer consists of lightweight, synthetic, moisture-wicking long underwear. A pair of sturdy pants (with shorts as a warm weather addition) and a sturdy shirt that will hold up to brush and rocks forms the second layer. The third layer consists of an insulating jacket or parka. Down is the lightest, most durable insulation, but it's hard to dry when wet. When you expect wet weather, consider a jacket insulated with a synthetic fill. Synthetic pile or fleece, which is marketed under a bewildering variety of trade names, is the warmest, driest insulator for very wet conditions. Even when soaked it can be wrung out and worn immediately. Finally, the fourth layer consists of a good set of rain pants and jacket with hood. If this outer layer is constructed from a waterproof and breathable fabric, it will do double duty as a wind shell.

Don't put up with being overheated or chilled. While hiking, stop to add or subtract layers as necessary to stay comfortable.

Food

Bring food on all but the shortest hikes. High calorie food keeps your energy levels high. You can make up sandwiches and other picnic items, or bring fruit, cheese, crackers, nuts, and drink mixes. I like to keep an athletic energy bar or two in my pack, so I always have something to eat even if I don't take anything else.

Although some companies make dehydrated food for backpacking and lightweight camping, such fare tends to be expensive. Many items found in supermarkets make good backpacking food at lower cost. I have been able to make many backpack trips with no more than 1.7 pounds of food per person per day. For breakfast, try low bulk cold cereals with powdered milk, hot cereals, dried fruit, breakfast bars, hot chocolate, tea, and coffee bags. For lunch, take munchies such as nuts, cheese, crackers, dried fruit, candy bars, athletic energy bars, dried soup, hard candy, beef or turkey jerky, sardines, and fruit-flavored drink mixes. For dinner, cook dried noodle- or rice-based dishes supplemented with margarine and a small can of tuna, turkey, or chicken.

Before leaving home, remove excess packaging such as cardboard boxes. Plastic bags with zipper closures make excellent food repackaging bags. Messy items should be double-bagged. Pack margarine and peanut butter in reliable, wide mouth plastic jars (available from outdoor suppliers). Unless you really trust the seal, put the container in a plastic bag too! Extra bags are useful during the trip for double-bagging messy trash such as sardine cans. Dedicate one or more nylon stuffsacks to food storage, and don't use them for anything else during the trip. The idea is to confine food odors as much as possible.

In camp, hang your food sacks from a 10- or 15-foot-high tree limb, if possible. This helps keep it away from scavengers, especially at night. The most foolproof technique is to divide your food into two equal sacks. Use a stone to toss the end of a piece of nylon cord over the limb well out from the trunk, then tie half your food to the end. Pull the food up to the limb, then tie your remaining food sack onto the cord as high as you can reach. Stuff the excess cord into the food sack, then use a stick to push the second sack several feet higher than your head. The first sack will act as a counterweight and descend a few feet, but it should remain at least as high as the second sack. In the morning, use a stick to pull down either of the sacks.

Water

On day hikes in the Great Basin, bring water from home—it is easier than purifying backcountry water sources. A few routes in the Snake Range have no reliable water sources during the dry season. Since each hiker may drink more than a gallon of water on a long, difficult, hot hike, it is imperative that you bring enough fluids with you.

Backcountry water sources in Great Basin National Park and the surrounding areas are not safe to drink. Appearance is no indication of safety; even sparkling clear water may contain dangerous parasites. Contamination comes from wild and domestic animals as well as increasing human use. Infections from contaminated water are uncomfortable and can be disabling. Giardiasis, for example, is a severe gastrointestinal infection caused by small cysts that can result in an emergency evacuation of the infected hiker. Giardiasis is spread by all mammals, including humans.

To avoid getting sick, purify all backcountry water sources. Iodine tablets, available from outdoor shops, are an effective wilderness water purification system. One iodine tablet per quart of water will kill nearly all dangerous organisms, including giardia cysts. Carefully read and follow the directions on the bottle to ensure effective use. In order to retain their potency, the tablets **must** be kept dry until used, and it's a good idea to discard opened bottles after each trip.

Since some hikers find the iodine taste objectionable, an iodine taste remover tablet is now available; it restores the original color and taste of the water without altering the iodine's effectiveness. The active biocidal agent is removed by these taste-remover tablets, so wait until the iodine tablets have had time to purify the water before adding them. Fruit and sport drinks containing ascorbic acid (vitamin C) have the same effect. Some people use such drink mixes to mask the taste of the iodine; if you do so, wait until the tablets have done their work before adding the drink mix.

Water filters are a popular alternative to iodine treatment, largely due to the better-tasting water they produce. They are heavier to carry than iodine tablets, and take longer to use. Filters cannot remove viruses because these are smaller than the pores in the filter elements, but some use active iodine elements to kill viruses. Water can also be purified by bringing it to a rolling boil. Heating water to boiling kills disease-causing organisms, which die well below the boiling point even at high altitude. Boiling's main drawbacks are that it uses extra fuel and gives water a flat taste. The latter problem is easily fixed by pouring the water back and forth between two containers several times. This restores dissolved air, which boiling removes.

The best water containers are plastic bottles with leak-proof caps, carried inside your pack. Another popular arrangement is a fanny pack with external bottle carriers. Metal canteens carried on your belt or on a shoulder strap are uncomfortable, and the water in them is quickly heated by the sun.

Necessary Accessories

Carry a knife when you hike. It is necessary for many routine tasks, such as cutting cord, and is vital for emergency fire building. Some hikers prefer the Swiss army type with scissors and other implements, while others like a simple, large bladed knife such as a folding hunter.

A good pair of sunglasses is essential when traveling in open areas during summer. Good glasses are optically correct and remove invisible ultraviolet and infrared light, reducing eyestrain and headaches. Ultraviolet protection is especially important at high altitude and on summer snowfields. The tag on the glasses will specify whether ultraviolet and infrared rays are filtered. Cheap sunglasses with no ultraviolet protection are worse than no sunglasses at all. They reduce visible light, causing the eye's iris to open and admit more of the damaging ultraviolet light. Excessive ultraviolet exposure causes snowblindness, a temporary but uncomfortable condition. Hikers who are dependent on prescription glasses or contact lenses should carry a spare pair of glasses. A hard plastic case will protect your expensive eyewear.

Sunscreen is another essential item. Lotions are rated by their Sun Protection Factor, or SPF, which approximates the amount of protection provided by the sunscreen as compared to unprotected skin. For example, a sunscreen rated at SPF 15 gives about fifteen times your natural protection. An SPF of 30 is not excessive for hiking in the mountains during summer. Few things can ruin a hike more completely than a bad sunburn.

A small first-aid kit will do for day hikes, but you'll definitely need a more complete kit for backpacking. Make sure that you get one intended specifically for wilderness sports. You may want to include a few repair items, such as spare bulbs and batteries for your flashlight, stove, and pack parts, and a sewing kit. At least one member of the party should have current first-aid skills. *Wilderness First Aid* and several other books (see Appendix C) are excellent sources of wilderness medical information.

A camera is probably the most common "extra" item carried on day hikes. Consider bringing a nylon ditty bag or plastic bag to protect it if rain is a possibility. Even the most waterproof packs can leak through seams and zippers. This advice also applies to any other items in your pack that could be damaged by water, such as maps.

Packs

A well-fitting, well-made day pack goes a long way toward making your hike a pleasant experience. Good packs are not cheap, but they will last a long time. Look for firm foam padding on the back panel and shoulder straps. Larger day packs usually have a waist belt, which may or may not be padded, and a reinforced bottom. Fanny packs are a popular alternative for shorter hikes. They are especially nice in warm weather, giving your back free air circulation. Their main drawback is limited capacity, which makes them unsuited for long hikes in remote areas or in changeable weather. Fanny packs work well for young children, enabling them to can carry a token amount and feel included in the group.

Packs for backpacking fall into two categories, internal frame and external frame. Internal frame packs have a frame built into the pack; the pack rides close to your body and balances well for cross-country hiking. External frame packs are usually made of aluminum tubing with a separately attached packbag. They are easier to pack and to overload for extended trips. They also give better back ventilation in hot weather. A good backpack of either type carefully distributes the load between your shoulders, back and hips, with most of the weight on your hips. Correct fit is critical. Models are now made specifically for men, women, and children, so getting a good fit is easier than ever.

A loaded pack means that you'll walk at a slower pace, especially uphill. Remember to allow for this when planning overnight trips versus day hikes. A walking stick can be helpful, especially at stream crossings or other places where the footing is uncertain. Such a stick can also be used to push brush and low branches out of the way, as a prop to turn a pack into a back rest, or to support a tarp for shelter from the weather.

Sleeping Bags and Pads

Your sleeping bag is one of the most important items in your pack. With a good one you'll get a comfortable night's sleep; with a poor bag, you're sure to have a miserable experience. The length of the manufacturer's warranty is a good indicator of quality. An occasional user may be happy with a backpacker-style mummy bag insulated with one of the current synthetic fills. Synthetic fills have advantages: they have a lower initial cost and retain some of their insulating ability when soaking wet. Still, high-quality down fill, though expensive, is unsurpassed in insulating capability for its weight. Since it is more durable, down is actually less expensive than synthetics over the lifetime of the bag. People who backpack often prefer down bags, which are more water-resistant than commonly thought (as anyone who has tried to wash a down bag by hand can tell you).

Sleeping bags are rated by temperature and sometimes by recommended seasons. A three-season bag is adequate for most backpackers. If you sleep warm, you may wish to get a lighter bag, and if you sleep cold, you'll probably prefer a warmer bag. Since lightweight sleeping bags don't provide much insulation or padding underneath, you'll also need a sleeping pad. The best type of pad currently available is the self-inflating, foam-filled air mattress. These are less prone to punctures than a traditional air mattress, are much warmer, and at least as comfortable. Closed-cell foam pads are a cheaper alternative. They insulate well but are not especially comfortable.

Shelter

Most hikers depend on a tent for shelter. Sound construction and high quality is important. A three-season, two-person dome or free-standing tent is the most versatile. Larger tents are more awkward to carry and require more spacious campsites. Nearly all tents use a separate waterproof fly over the tent canopy, which provides rain protection and also allows moisture to escape from within the tent. Small children can share a tent with their parents, but as they get older, kids often enjoy setting up their own.

Some experienced hikers avoid the weight and expense of a tent by carrying a nylon tarp with a separate groundsheet. A tarp provides good weather protection if set up properly and is versatile enough to use as shade or a windbreak during lunch stops. Using a tarp effectively does take some practice. Also, a tarp provides no protection from mosquitoes and other insects!

TRIP PLANNING

Many local outdoor shops are staffed by people who use the gear that they sell and are willing to share their knowledge with you. These shops are a valuable resource that is worth supporting. If you can't find a good local shop, then look into mail-order companies. There are several reputable catalog companies; check ads in the outdoor magazines for addresses and phone numbers.

Maps are essential for trip planning and should be obtained in advance of the trip. Guidebooks allow you to learn about an area more quickly than you could with maps alone. Once you are comfortable with an area and have done many of the hikes in the guidebooks, you will be able to plan your own hikes using maps and information from other hikers to help you.

When planning a backpacking trip, consider alternatives to traditional campsites. Dry camping—camping with just the water you carry—is a valuable skill with many advantages. Dry camping virtually eliminates the possibility of contaminating wilderness streams and lakes. You can avoid heavily used campsites and their camp-robbing animal attendants, such as skunks, mice, gray jays, and insects. Dry camping opens up many beautiful, uncrowded camp locations.

The technique is simple. Use a collapsible water container to pick up water at the last reliable source you cross or reach during the day, then use minimum water for camp chores. Plan your route so that you pass a reliable water source each day of the trip or, better, late in the afternoon and again first thing in the morning. Note that certain areas in Great Basin National Park are closed to camping; these include the Wheeler Day Use Area, all bristlecone pine groves, and all alpine lakes.

Maps

Several different types of maps are available for wilderness navigation. Topographic maps are the most useful because they show the elevation and shape of the land through the use of contour lines. The Snake Range is covered by a series of maps in the 7.5-minute quadrangle series published by the U.S. Geological Survey (USGS). Each hike description in this book lists the USGS topographic maps that cover that particular hike. The USGS maps are produced from aerial photos to high standards of accuracy. At a scale of 1:24,000 (2.6 inches to the mile) and printed in sheets that cover about 7 by 9 miles, these are usually the most detailed maps available. The only catch is that the USGS can't update the maps all that often, so details such as trails and roads may be out of date. USGS maps are sold at the park visitor center, and are also available by mail order from the USGS map distribution center in Denver. (See Appendix A for the current address.) Request a free Nevada index and catalog of topographic maps.

As of this writing, Earthwalk Press produces a topographic map of Great Basin National Park that shows many of the area trails. This map is handy because it shows the entire park on one sheet, though with less detail than the USGS maps. It's available in a waterproof, recycled-paper edition at the park visitor center.

The Forest Service publishes the Humboldt National Forest–Ely Ranger District map. This map shows the forest road system at a scale of 1:126,720 (0.5 inch to the mile). It also shows official road numbers that appear on road signs, which makes the map valuable for exploring the more remote sections of the Snake Range. This map is available from the Ely Ranger Station in Ely (see Appendix A).

Map reading is a skill that requires practice, but it pays off in increased safety in the backcountry. The best way to learn how to read a map is to get a map of an area that you already know. Go to a place where you can get an overview of the terrain and spend some time relating what you see to the map symbols. Before entering the Great Basin backcountry, study the maps to become familiar with the general lay of the land. Trail signs, even within the park, may be vandalized or inaccurate. Stay aware of your location at all times, and use the trail signs as confirmation. While hiking, refer to the map often and locate yourself in reference to visible landmarks. If you do this consistently, without relying on trail signs, you will never become lost.

Compasses

Always carry a reliable, liquid-filled compass so that you can determine directions in dense forest or bad weather. Make sure that it is in working condition before you set out. Because backcountry navigation consists primarily of map reading, your compass will probably languish in your pack for years before you use it! When you finally do need it, you will need it badly—not a good time to find out that the needle has fallen off.

Global Positioning System

The satellite navigation system maintained by the U.S. Department of Defense makes it possible to find your location nearly anywhere on earth. The Global Positioning System (GPS) consists of a set of twenty-four satellites orbiting 12,000 miles above the earth. Low-cost, portable receivers are available that are designed specifically for ground navigation. The readout shows your position within about 330 feet (100 meters). Weather conditions do not affect the accuracy of GPS, but the receiver must have a clear view of the sky. This means that dense forest, narrow canyons, or poor satellite geometry can prevent an accurate fix.

A GPS unit is no substitute for a good map and a reliable compass. Keep in mind that the unit is useless if the batteries die; take spares! When buying a unit for hiking, make sure it uses the Universal Transverse Mercator (UTM) coordinate system, as well as latitude and longitude. UTM is found on USGS topographic maps, and many find it easier to use than the latitude and longitude system. Any map accurate enough for wilderness navigation will have at least the latitudinal and longitudinal coordinates.

Walking

Walking in wild country is not just a matter of "picking 'em up and putting 'em down!" Most novice hikers try to go too fast, then find themselves out of breath and stopping frequently. Hikers who travel in a group should move at a speed that allows easy conversation among all members. Long hikes, especially uphill sections, should be paced so that rest breaks are needed only about once an hour. That's not to say that you shouldn't stop at scenic viewpoints or when you find something interesting. But if you find yourself taking a great many breaks, you're probably going too fast. Keep rest stops short so that you don't become chilled. It's harder to get going after a long break.

As you walk, always pay attention to the stretch of ground immediately in front of you. Hazards such as spiny plants, overhanging sharp branches, and sunbathing rattlesnakes are easy to miss if you only have eyes for the scenery. On the other hand, daydreaming is an important part of hiking. There are always sections of trail that don't grab your attention. An experienced hiker can let her or his mind wander but still pay attention to the trail underfoot. A veteran hiker can focus on aspects of the environment, such as birdsong or identifying trees from a distance by their general shape. Either technique lets the miles pass almost unnoticed.

Hikers traveling with young children should set extremely modest goals. A day hike of a few hundred yards may be far enough for the youngest trekkers. In even a small area, children can find all sorts of interesting things that their parents never notice. Introduce your children to short day hikes at an early age, gradually lengthening the distance as they grow older and their stamina and desire to hike increase. Their first overnight hikes can be kept short, as they should be for any novice hiker. Once a child is old enough to carry a pack, keep it light. If you progressively introduce your children to backpacking, by the time they are energetic teenagers they'll be so addicted to hiking that you may be able persuade them to carry some of your own load. (Good luck!)

Trail Courtesy

Never cut switchbacks on trails. Shortcutting actually takes more physical effort than staying on the trail. It also increases erosion and the need for trail maintenance. Give horses and other pack animals the right of way, by stepping off-trail on the downhill side. Greet the riders or talk in a normal tone of voice before the animals reach you, to let them know you're there; don't make sudden movements or loud noises, which can spook an animal.

Mountain bikes are not allowed on trails or in the backcountry in Great Basin National Park or the Mount Moriah Wilderness. You may encounter bikes outside these areas, however. Since bikes are less maneuverable than you, it's polite to step aside so the riders can pass without having to veer off the trail.

Smokers should light up only at a bare spot or rock ledge, then make certain that all smoking materials are out before continuing. Please note that most cigarette butts are **not** biodegradable—they should be packed out with the rest of your garbage. Never smoke or light any kind of fire on windy days or when the fire danger is high, because wildfires will start easily and spread explosively.

Dogs are not allowed on trails in the national park. Although dogs are allowed in the Humboldt National Forest and Mount Moriah Wilderness Area, they are best left at home. Barking dogs disturb other hikers, and their presence places unnecessary stress on wildlife. If you do bring your dog, you must maintain control of your animal. Bring and use a leash.

Weather

During summer, heat can be a hazard, especially at lower elevations. In hot weather, each hiker will need at least a gallon of water every day. To avoid dehydration, drink more water than you need to merely quench your thirst. Sport drinks that replace electrolytes are useful. Protection from both the heat and the sun is important. During hot weather, plan hikes at higher elevations, or hike early in the day to avoid afternoon heat.

In the Great Basin, thunderstorms occur regularly during summer. Usually towering cumulus clouds appear first, warning of the thunderstorms and lightning to follow. In thunderstorm season, plan your hikes to avoid high ridges and peaks during the afternoon. If a storm forms, get off exposed ridges and stay away from lone trees. If lightning strikes your immediate area, crouch on a sleeping pad or other insulating object, keeping contact with the ground to a minimum. The idea is to reduce your exposure to the ground currents caused by a lightning bolt; these spread out from the point of the actual strike.

Year-round, hikers should avoid continuous exposure to chilling weather, which may subtly lower body temperature and cause sudden collapse from hypothermia. Cool winds, especially when paired with rain, are the most dangerous. A life-threatening condition, hypothermia may be completely prevented by wearing enough layers of clothing to avoid chilling, and by eating and drinking regularly so that your body produces heat. Snow may fall at any time of year on the Snake Range. Be prepared for it by bringing more layers of warm clothing than you think you will need. During the wet season, use synthetic garments made of polypropylene or polyester fibers, since these fibers retain their insulating ability when wet better than any natural fiber, including wool.

Insects and Their Kin

Insects are not a major hazard in the Snake Range. Mosquitoes are rare. Scorpions are found nearly everywhere, but the species found here are not especially hazardous. Other insects, such as bees, wasps, and the like, also give non-threatening but painful stings. An exception to this applies to people who have a known allergic reaction to specific insect stings. Since this reaction can develop rapidly and be life-threatening, such people should check with their doctors to see if desensitization treatment is recommended. They should also carry prescription-strength insect-sting kits.

Snakes

Rattlesnakes are uncommon at the park's higher elevations, but they may be encountered in the lower country. They can be avoided easily because they usually warn off intruders by rattling well before a person is within striking range. Since rattlesnakes can strike as far as approximately half their body length, avoid placing your hands and feet in areas that you cannot see, and walk several feet away from rock overhangs and shady ledges. Bites usually occur on the feet or ankles, so ankle-high hiking boots and loose-fitting long pants will prevent most injuries. Snakes prefer surfaces at about 80 degrees F (27 degrees C), so during hotter weather they prefer the shade of bushes or rock overhangs, and in cooler weather they will be found on open ground. Don't confuse common, nonpoisonous bull snakes with rattlesnakes. For your own safety, never handle or tease any snake.

Wildlife

Wild animals normally leave hikers alone unless they have been molested or provoked. Do not feed any wild animal, since an animal that is not wary of humans will rapidly get used to handouts and then vigorously defend its new food source. Around camp, problems with rodents can be avoided by hanging your food from rocks or trees. Even the toughest pack can be wrecked by a determined mouse or squirrel that has all night to work.

Plants

Spiny plants are a notable hazard in the Snake Range. Always watch where you place your hands and feet. Spines can be removed with a pair of tweezers, a good item to have in your first-aid kit. Stinging nettles are harder to deal with because the plants' irritating hairs are so fine. Apply a strip of adhesive tape over the affected area, then remove it to pull out the nettle hairs. Poison ivy may be found in the region's lower canyons; it is easily recognized by its shiny leaves, which grow in groups of three. If you accidentally make contact with poison ivy, calamine lotion may help relieve the itching.

Never eat any plant, unless you positively know what you are doing.

Rescue

Anyone entering remote country should be self-sufficient and prepared to take care of emergencies such as equipment failure and minor medical problems. Very rarely, circumstances may give rise to a life-threatening situation that requires an emergency evacuation or a search effort. In Great Basin National Park, the National Park Service is responsible for search and rescue; in all other areas covered by this book, it's the White Pine County Sheriff's Office in Ely. The Humboldt National Forest rangers cooperate with the local sheriff's department and may also be contacted in the event of an emergency.

Always leave word of your hiking plans with a reliable individual. For backpack trips, provide that person with a written itinerary. The responsible person should be advised to contact the appropriate authority if you are overdue. In your instructions, allow extra time for routine delays.

Don't count on a cellular phone for communications in the backcountry. The cellular phone system is dependent upon a closely spaced network of short-range radio transmitters designed for use in cities and populated areas. Cell phone coverage is not continuous in rural areas and may be nonexistent in wilderness. Even if you can alert authorities to your problem, you will have a better chance of surviving until rescuers arrive if you are self-sufficient.

LEAVE NO TRACE

There are too many of us in the backcountry now to support outdated practices such as cutting live trees or plants of any kind, blazing or carving initials on trees or rocks, picking wildflowers, and building rock campfire rings. Responsible hikers follow three no-trace precepts that leave the wilderness as untouched as possible:

3 Falcon Principles of Leave No Trace

- **Leave with everything you carried in**
- **Leave no sign of your visit**
- **Leave the landscape as you found it**

Additionally, hikers should never disturb ruins or other old sites and artifacts. These sites are protected by the National Historic Preservation Act and the Archeological Resources Preservation Act, which are intended to preserve our historic and prehistoric heritage. Archaeologists study artifacts in place because the setting reveals more information than the artifact alone. Once a site is disturbed, another piece of the puzzle is gone forever.

Low-Impact Camping

To avoid scarring the land, camp on reasonably level sites with dry, sandy soil, bare rock, or forest duff. Avoid fragile, easily damaged sites such as grassy meadows, lakeshores, and stream banks. Select a site that's screened from trails, meadows, and other campsites. As a rule of thumb, camp out of sight and sound of others, respecting their desire for wilderness solitude. Start looking for a campsite at least a couple of hours before dark. Campsites become harder to find as the group size increases—a good reason to avoid groups larger than five or six people.

If bad weather threatens, look for a campsite sheltered from wind and blowing rain, preferably with natural drainage and an absorbent surface such as forest duff or sand. Heavy forest provides protection from rain at the beginning of a storm, but trees can drip for hours after the rain stops. Never dig drainage ditches or excavate dirt to level a campsite; these obsolete practices cause erosion and severe damage. A slight slope will keep groundwater from pooling under your tent. Modern sleeping pads make it possible to camp on gravel or even rock slabs in comfort. During hot weather, look for shade, especially from the morning sun. In heavy forest, check overhead for "widowmakers"—large dead branches that may break off and crash down.

Certain areas in Great Basin National Park are closed to camping; these include the Wheeler Day Use Area, all bristlecone pine groves, and all lakes. Other areas may be closed as needed; check with the visitor center for the latest information. Land managers sometimes close other areas to camping or entry to allow it to recover from heavy use. Please respect these closures.

Campfires

Campfires are prohibited above 10,000 feet in Great Basin National Park, and bristlecone pine should not be burned at any elevation. Many of the trees in the park are thousands of years old and grow very slowly. In the Great Basin's arid climate, dead trees and downed wood may last for hundreds of years. Researchers can use these old plant remains. They correlate tree ring data between living and downed trees and, in doing so, learn details of climate changes valuable for understanding today's weather patterns. Show respect for alpine life, which started here at the dawn of human civilization, by not building fires at high elevation anywhere in the Snake Range. I strongly recommend using a lightweight backpacker's stove for cooking.

There are no specific rules against campfires in the Mount Moriah Wilderness Area or the Humboldt National Forest, except during periods of high fire danger. At lower elevations in the forest, it's possible to enjoy a campfire responsibly. Use an established campfire ring if one is available. Otherwise, look for a site in gravel, sand, or bare soil. The ground should be naturally bare around your fire site to prevent the fire from spreading. Dig a shallow firepit, heaping dirt around the edges to form a wind and fire break. **Do not use stones**, because they become permanently blackened.

Collect firewood only by gathering dead wood from the ground. There's no need to carry a saw or an ax; if you need such implements to collect wood, then it's too scarce to justify building a campfire except in an emergency. Keep your fire small to conserve wood and minimize ashes. Large fires escape easily and have a nasty tendency to throw sparks on your expensive equipment. Don't burn trash in your campfire. Many paper packages are lined with **aluminum foil, which does not burn** in any campfire, no matter how hot. Plastic also does not burn well, and may give off highly toxic fumes. Unfortunately, plenty of old firepits are full of charred plastic and sparkling bits of aluminum to prove the point.

When you are ready to leave camp, make sure your campfire is cold by adding water or dirt to the coals and stirring until there is no visible smoke or heat. Then check the ashes with your bare hand. Finally, cover the firepit with the dirt you took from it originally, and scatter any remaining wood. After a short time, your fire site will look natural again.

Trash and Personal Waste

If you carried it in, you can also carry it out. Lightweight food that has been carefully repacked to eliminate excess packaging produces little trash, even after a week or more in the backcountry. Avoid burying food or trash, because after you leave animals will find it by smell, dig it up, and scatter it all over the place. Don't feed wild creatures; they will become dependent on human food, which is not good for them and can lead to winter starvation. Also, animals used to human contact become more aggressive in seeking out food sources, which leads to unpleasant human/wildlife encounters.

Disposing of personal waste correctly is critical. Naturally occurring diseases such as giardiasis are aggravated by poor human sanitation. Fortunately, wilderness sanitation is mostly common sense. If restroom or outhouse facilities are available, use them! Their presence means that the human population of the area is too large for the soil's natural disposal systems. In the backcountry, select a site at least 100 yards from streams, lakes, springs, and dry washes, avoiding barren, sandy soil if possible. Next, dig a small "cat-hole" about 6 inches into the organic layer of the soil. (Some people carry a small plastic trowel for this purpose.) When finished, refill the hole, leaving the site as natural as possible. Land managers now recommend that all toilet paper be carried out. Use double plastic bags, with a small amount of baking soda to absorb odor.

USING THIS GUIDE

Many of the trails in Great Basin National Park are unmaintained, faint, obscured by cattle trails, or confused by old jeep tracks. Except on the Wheeler Peak, Alpine Lakes, Bristlecone–Glacier, Baker Lake, and Lexington Arch trails (which are well-signed, well-traveled, and easy to follow), hikers should carry either USGS or Earthwalk· Press topographic maps, and be familiar with map reading and land navigation. Because many of the trails in the Snake Range are long and difficult, with considerable elevation change, I have made an extra effort to describe the area's easiest hikes in this book.

Each hike description contains the following information:

Hike number and name: We list each trail's name as it is most commonly known. The hike number is also shown on the Overview Map at the front of the book.

Special attractions: Reasons for doing the hike.

Type of trail: Out and back hikes are two-way hikes where hikers return by backtracking their route. Loop hikes start and end at the same trailhead, but avoid retracing the trail (though there may be some repeated sections). Shuttle hikes are one-way hikes starting and ending at different trailheads. You will have to leave a vehicle at both trailheads, or arrange for pickup at the exit trailhead.

Type of trip: Day hike or backpack trip. Some day hikes can be expanded into easy backpack trips, and ambitious hikers may cover a backpack trip in one day. A few areas are closed to backpacking, so read the full hike description before you plan your route.

Total distance: In miles, with kilometers in parentheses. For out and back

Alpine meadows below Johnson Pass.

hikes, this distance is a one-way distance that does not include the return leg. For loops and shuttle hikes, this is also the one-way distance.

Difficulty: Hikes are rated easy, moderate, or difficult. This is a subjective rating but, in general, easy hikes can be done by nearly anyone and take a few hours at most. Moderate hikes take all or most of a day and require average physical abilities. Difficult hikes are long with significant elevation change, requiring a full day or several days to accomplish. These hikes should be attempted only by experienced hikers in good physical condition.

Elevation change: The total altitude change in feet, with meters in parentheses.

Elevation graph: For hikes with significant elevation change only. Each graph shows a profile view of the elevations of the hike, measured in feet.

Time required: A highly subjective estimate of the number of hours or days required for an average hiker to walk the trail. I've tried to err on the conservative side.

Water: A mention of any known, reliable sources along the route. Remember that all backcountry water should be purified.

Maps: The appropriate USGS 7.5-minute topographic quadrangle is always listed, along with the Earthwalk Press and Forest Service maps if they are useful.

Finding the trailhead: Driving directions are given from the town of Baker, Nevada, for all the hikes in this book. Distances are given in miles, with kilometers in parentheses.

Key points: This is a listing of key points such as trail junctions and important landmarks along the hike. You should be able to follow the route easily by referring to this section. Distances are given from the start of the hike in miles, with kilometers in parentheses.

The hike: Here, in narrative form, I describe the hike in detail. Each description may include interesting facts of natural and human history. The description refers to landmarks rather than distances wherever possible.

Alpine phlox on stone, Bald Mountain.

Author's Recommendations

Easy day hikes	Strawberry Creek– Osceola Ditch	Alpine Lakes Lehman Cave
Early season hikes	Osceola Tunnel Osceola Ditch Interpretive Trail Mountain View Nature Trail	Pole Canyon Can Young Canyon
Very easy day hikes for parents with small children	Osceola Tunnel Osceola Ditch Interpretive Trail Mountain View Nature Trail	Snake Creek
First night in the wilderness	Pole Canyon	
Long day hikes	Lehman Creek Johnson Lake Baker and Johnson lakes Timber Creek–South Fork Baker Creek	Bristlecone-Glacier Trail South Fork Big Wash
Hikes for photographers	Bald Mountain Alpine Lakes Johnson Lake Wheeler Peak	Bristlecone-Glacier Trail Lexington Arch
Hikes with lots of side trips and exploring	Baker and Johnson lakes Timber Creek–South Fork Baker Creek Johnson Lake	Smith Creek Hendrys Creek
Hikes for peak baggers	Bald Mountain Wheeler Peak Hendrys Creek Big Canyon	
Hikes for backpackers	Johnson Lake Dead Lake South Fork Big Wash Timber Creek–South Fork Baker Creek	Baker and Johnson lakes Hendrys Creek

Great Basin National Park

1 Osceola Tunnel

Special attractions:	An easy walk to a historic, hand-dug tunnel.
Type of trail:	Out and back.
Type of trip:	Day hike.
Total distance:	1.4 miles (2.2 km).
Difficulty:	Easy.
Elevation change:	From 8,000 to 8,240 feet (2,430 to 2,510 m).
Time required:	1 hour.
Water:	None.
Maps:	USGS Windy Peak; Humboldt National Ranger District.

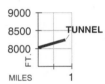

Finding the trailhead: From Baker, drive 5 miles (8 km) northwest on Nevada Highway 487, then turn left on U.S. Highway 6/50. Go 3.3 miles (5.3 km), then turn left on an unsigned, paved road that goes toward a maintenance facility. After 0.3 mile (0.5 km), just before reaching the facility, turn right on the signed dirt road to Strawberry Creek. Continue another 5.2 miles (8.4 km) to a Road Closed sign on the right, next to a lone tree. This point, in the middle of the meadow at the head of Strawberry Creek, is the trailhead.

Key points in miles (km):
    0.0 (0.0)   Trailhead at Road Closed sign.
    0.7 (1.1)   Tunnel.

The hike: This is an easy, enjoyable walk with nice views of upper Strawberry Valley and the beautiful, forested slopes of Bald Mountain. The trail follows an old, closed jeep track across the meadow and up the hillside to the pass visible to the northwest. When you reach the pass, go through the gate (please leave it as you found it) and walk down the road a short distance north. Look for mine tailings below to the left, then head down the short slope. This is the exit point for the Osceola Tunnel, which went through the rock under the pass you just walked over. The tunnel allowed water from the Eastern Osceola Ditch to get to this point without having to contour miles around the hill to the east. Remains of the ditch are visible several hundred feet lower on the hillsides to the northwest. The water flowed

Northern entrance to the Osceola Tunnel.

Osceola Tunnel • Strawberry Creek–Osceola Ditch

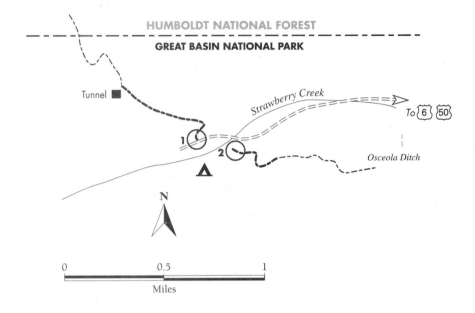

from the tunnel down a wooden chute for about 400 vertical feet (122 m) before pouring into the ditch again. (For more details on the ditch, see Hike 3, Osceola Ditch Interpretive Trail.)

2   Strawberry Creek–Osceola Ditch

See Map on Page 34

Special attractions:	An easy walk to a historic water diversion site, with an optional longer hike.
Type of trail:	Out and back.
Type of trip:	Day hike.
Total distance:	1 mile (1.6 km); longer optional.
Difficulty:	Easy.
Elevation change:	From 7,960 to 8,200 feet (2,425 to 2,500 m).
Time required:	1 hour (longer optional).
Water:	Strawberry Creek.
Maps:	USGS Windy Peak; Humboldt National Forest–Ely Ranger District.

Finding the trailhead: From Baker, drive 5 miles (8 km) northwest on Nevada Highway 487, then turn left on U.S. Highway 6/50. Go 3.3 miles (5.3 km), then turn left on the unsigned, paved road that goes toward a maintenance facility. At 0.3 mile (0.5 km), just before reaching the facility, turn right onto the signed dirt road to Strawberry Creek. Continue 5 miles (8 km), then turn left before the road crosses the creek a final time. Go 0.1 mile (0.2 km) to a primitive campsite at the end of the road. This is the trailhead.

Strawberry Creek is a scenic and accessible area in the northern section of the Park.

35

Key points in miles (km):
  0.0 (0.0)   Trailhead at the primitive campsite.
  0.5 (0.8)   Osceola Ditch.

The hike: From the trailhead, walk back down the road a few yards to the old, closed jeep trail that climbs the hill to the right (south). Follow this road up the hillside, through an aspen grove, and up a switchback. When you come to a junction, turn left (east) and follow the old road up to the abandoned Osceola Ditch. This vantage point has fine views of Strawberry Valley. You can also see the Osceola Ditch route at the head of the valley. This viewpoint is your destination for this easy hike but, if you desire, you can follow the old road east along the ditch for several miles. For more information on the history of the ditch, see Hike 3, Osceola Ditch Interpretive Trail.

Section of the abandoned Osceola Ditch near the Interpretive Trail.

3 Osceola Ditch Interpretive Trail

Special attractions: An easy interpretive trail to a historic site.
Type of trail: Out and back.
Type of trip: Day hike.
Total distance: 0.6 mile (1 km).
Difficulty: Easy.
Elevation change: None; trail is at 8,400 feet (2,560 m).
Time required: 0.5 hour.
Water: None.
Maps: USGS Windy Peak.

Finding the trailhead: From Baker, drive 5 miles (8 km) west on Nevada Highway 488. Just after passing the boundary of Great Basin National Park, turn right on the paved, signed Wheeler Peak Scenic Drive. Continue 4.6 miles (7.4 km) to the signed Osceola Ditch Interpretive Site, and park on the right side of the highway.

Key points in miles (km):
0.0 (0.0)   Trailhead.
0.3 (0.5)   Osceola Ditch.

Osceola Ditch Interpretive Trail • Lehman Creek

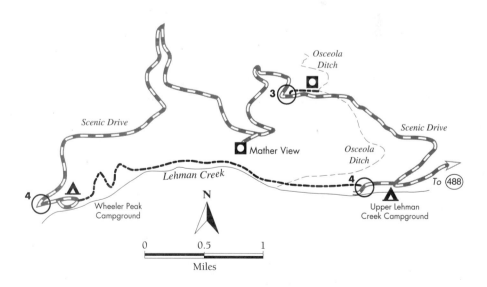

The hike: A sign at the Osceola Ditch Interpretive Site trailhead briefly explains the history and purpose of the Osceola Ditch. The trail follows a drainage downhill through the woods a short distance to reach the remains of the ditch, which contours along the hillside. When it was operational, the ditch ran 18 miles (29 km) along the Snake Range to deliver water from Lehman Creek, on the east side of the range, to the town of Osceola on the west side.

Why such a massive undertaking? In a word, gold. In 1872, prospectors discovered gold northwest of the present Great Basin National Park. Within five years, miners found gold placer deposits and activity gained momentum. Placer mining can be done by hand with a gold pan, but for large-scale mining it was more efficient to direct the force of water. In the hydraulic mining process, a jet of water is aimed at a hillside to wash out the gravel and dislocate any gold that might be present. The water and gravel mix is then run through a series of sluices, which separate out the heavier gold. The catch is that a large supply of water is required.

In 1884–1885, a 16-mile (26-km) ditch was built south along the west slopes of the Snake Range to capture water from several creeks and bring it to Osceola. But the amount of water from the west-side streams was disappointing and the mines were able to operate for only about two hours a day. A second ditch, this time diverting water from larger streams on the east side of the range, was proposed. Though the new ditch would cross more difficult terrain and would be expensive, the amount of gold that miners thought they could recover with more water seemed to indicate that the venture would be profitable. Work started in September 1889, and the ditch was finished in July of the following year. Several hundred men with pack animals worked on the project, and three sawmills ran full time to provide lumber. In places where the route traversed cliffs and steep rocky slopes, wooden flumes and chutes were constructed, totaling 11,600 feet (3,536 m). A 632-foot (193-m) tunnel was blasted through the ridge north of Strawberry Creek. The cost was $108,223, only a few thousand dollars more than originally estimated.

At first, gold production near Osceola increased, but there were problems with the new ditch. In the end, lawsuits over water rights, water theft, and leaking flumes caused the Eastern Osceola Ditch to fail to deliver as much water as anticipated. Dry years, starting in 1893, cut further into the water supply, and by 1901 the ditch was abandoned. Mining activity in the area had almost completely ceased by 1905.

4   Lehman Creek

See Map on Page 37

Special attractions:	A scenic hike along an alpine creek.
Type of trail:	Out and back or shuttle.
Type of trip:	Day hike.
Total distance:	8 miles (12.9 km) out and back; 4 miles (6.5 km) with a shuttle.
Difficulty:	Difficult.
Elevation change:	From 7,750 to 9,820 feet (2,360 to 2,990 m).
Time required:	5 hours out and back, 3 hours with a shuttle.
Water:	Upper Lehman Campground, Wheeler Peak Campground, Lehman Creek.
Maps:	USGS Windy Peak; Earthwalk Press Great Basin National Park.

Finding the trailhead: From Baker, drive west 5 miles (8 km) on Nevada Highway 488, the park approach road. Just past the park entrance, turn right (north) on the signed, paved Wheeler Peak Scenic Drive. Continue 2.4 miles (3.7 km) to Upper Lehman Campground. Turn left at the second camp-

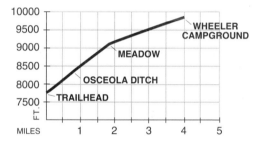

ground entrance, then drive to the signed trailhead. The trailhead is on the right just before the road enters the campground loop.

If you have two vehicles, you can do a shuttle to make this an all-down-hill hike. To reach the Wheeler Peak Campground trailhead from Upper Lehman Creek Campground, continue up the scenic drive 9.6 miles (15.5 km) to the Bristlecone parking area near Wheeler Peak Campground. Walk east through the campground to the start of the trail.

Key points in miles (km):
   0.0 (0.0)   Trailhead.
   0.7 (1.1)   Osceola Ditch.
   1.7 (2.7)   Meadow with views.
   4.0 (6.5)   Wheeler Peak Campground.

The hike: The Lehman Creek trail is well maintained and easy to follow as it climbs steadily through a mountain mahogany thicket, away from the creek. After a while the trail returns to the creek; watch for the remains of the old Osceola Ditch, which the trail crosses. You can follow the ditch to the creek, but there is no trace of the original wooden structure used to divert the creek water.

Sage meadow along the Lehman Creek Trail.

After crossing the old ditch, the trail stays near the creek in a cool, dense fir and aspen forest. It then swings away from the creek and climbs a ridge to enter a meadow at about 9,100 feet (2,370 m) with good views of Jeff Davis and Wheeler peaks. Above the meadows, the trail comes near the creek briefly before swinging away and climbing a final slope in a wide switchback.

The signed trailhead that marks your destination point is at the east end of Wheeler Peak Campground. If you want to combine this hike with the Alpine Lakes Loop or other trails that start from the campground, continue uphill to the west end of the campground and the signed trailhead. Otherwise, return to Upper Lehman Campground the way you came.

---

5   Bald Mountain

See Map on Page 45

Special attractions:	A hike on trails and cross-country to an easy summit; offers fine views of Wheeler Peak and Jeff Davis Peak.
Type of trail:	Out and back.
Type of trip:	Day hike.
Total distance:	5.6 miles (9 km).
Difficulty:	Moderate.
Elevation change:	From 9,960 to 11,562 feet (3,035 to 3,524 m).
Time required:	5 hours.
Water:	Wheeler Peak Campground.
Maps:	USGS Windy Peak.

Finding the trailhead: From Baker, drive 5 miles west on Nevada Highway 488. Just after passing the Great Basin National Park boundary, turn right on the paved, signed Wheeler Peak Scenic Drive. Continue 12 miles to the signed Bristlecone Trailhead, just before the road enters Wheeler Peak Campground.

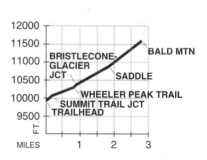

Key points in miles (km):

0.0 (0.0)	Trailhead.
0.2 (0.3)	Junction with Bristlecone-Glacier Trail; turn right.
0.7 (1.1)	Junction with Summit Trail; turn left.
0.8 (1.3)	Junction with Wheeler Peak Trail; turn right.
1.8 (2.9)	Wheeler Saddle; go north, cross-country.
2.8 (4.5)	Bald Mountain.

Alpine tundra on Bald Mountain.

The hike: Bald Mountain is much easier to climb than Wheeler Peak, and may appeal to hikers or peak baggers who have limited time. Start from the trailhead at Wheeler Peak Campground by walking across the road to the Alpine Lakes Trailhead. The trail crosses Lehman Creek on a footbridge, then climbs gradually through dense forest. Turn right at the junction with the Bristlecone–Glacier Trail. The trail crosses the creek again, then enters a series of alpine meadows. At the signed junction with the Summit Trail turn left.

After a short distance, turn right on the Wheeler Peak Trail. Stay on this trail until it reaches Wheeler Saddle, almost directly above Stella Lake. Now turn right (north), and walk cross-country up the easy ridge. Here, right at timberline, stunted Engelmann spruce and bristlecone pine trees are the last outposts of the forest. Some of the trees have formed classic *krummholz*, a term that refers to the low, matted forms taken by timberline trees. In winter, snow covers the krummholz, insulating the foliage from the bitter wind and driven snow.

Our route continues right up the broad ridge, climbing gently to the rounded summit of Bald Mountain at 11,562 feet (3,524 m). The view takes in the north slopes of the southern Snake Range, the Mount Moriah massif in the northern Snakes, and the plunging cliffs on Wheeler and Jeff Davis peaks.

6   Wheeler Peak

Special attractions:	Highest summit in the Snake Range and second highest in Nevada.
Type of trail:	Out and back.
Type of trip:	Day hike.
Total distance:	8 miles (12.9 km).
Difficulty:	Difficult.
Elevation change:	From 10,160 to 13,063 feet (3,100 to 3,982 m).
Time required:	6 to 8 hours.
Water:	Wheeler Peak Campground.
Maps:	USGS Wheeler Peak, Windy Peak; Earthwalk Press Great Basin National Park.

Finding the trailhead: From Baker, drive west 5 miles (8 km) on the Great Basin National Park entrance road (Nevada Highway 488), then turn right (north) on Wheeler Peak Scenic Drive. Continue 11.5 miles (18.5 km) to the signed Summit Trailhead, which is about 0.5 mile from the end of the road.

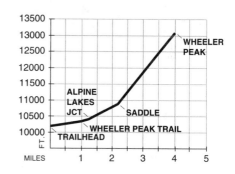

Key points in miles (km):

0.0 (0.0)   Trailhead.
1.0 (1.7)   Junction with Alpine Lakes Trail; turn right.
1.2 (1.9)   Junction with Wheeler Peak Trail; turn right.
2.2 (3.5)   Wheeler Saddle.
4.0 (6.5)   Wheeler Peak.

The hike: Follow the Summit Trail as it climbs gradually southwest through stands of aspen along the southern slopes of Bald Mountain. Openings in the forest provide outstanding views of Wheeler and Jeff Davis peaks. The Alpine Lakes Trail joins from the left; continue a short distance west, then turn sharply right on the signed Wheeler Peak Trail.

The trail ascends the southeast slopes of Bald Mountain through a broad meadow with more great views of the big peaks to the north. Before long the trail switches back to the south—please do not cut this switchback, since the alpine vegetation is very fragile. Continue along the slope until you gain the ridge crest. Stunted and gnarled limber pine and Engelmann spruce, the last vestiges of forest, struggle to survive at treeline. Views are commanding to both east and west. The clear, shallow waters of Stella Lake are visible, well below, to the east. Above this point, the trail stays above timberline and exposes hikers to high-altitude weather. Be certain the weather

Storm clouds over Wheeler Peak.

is good and that you have warm clothing, and especially a wind shell, before you continue.

Follow the trail as it climbs south up the broad north ridge of Wheeler Peak. The ridge narrows and allows a short respite from the climb at about 11,800 feet (3,600 m). The trail steepens as it begins the final ascent. Views down the west slopes are stunning; the entire 7,000-foot sweep of the west ridge is visible from the summit to the floor of Spring Valley. Use care early in the season, when large snowfields may block parts of the trail. These snowfields may be very dangerous, since the slippery snow ends above high cliffs to the north. If necessary to avoid snow, deviate to the right (south) of the trail.

Surprisingly, there are small patches of alpine plants and flowers growing in sheltered areas all along the ascent, even at the summit, which is 2,000 feet above timberline. Plants growing above treeline must adapt to the arctic environment of strong wind and severe cold. Views from the summit extend far into Utah to the east, and across a wide sweep of Nevada to the west. To the north, the bulk of Mount Moriah dominates the northern Snake Range.

Rock shelters have been built here by hikers for protection from the wind. Along the summit ridge to the east, you will spot several platforms. Look carefully and you will see that the construction was more than casual. These were tent platforms built by the Wheeler Survey, which occupied the summit during summer and fall for four years, starting in 1881. The Survey's purpose was to precisely measure the distance and direction to other mountain peaks. This work, coordinated with other federal surveys, resulted in the first accurate topographic survey of the entire continent.

Bald Mountain • Wheeler Peak • Alpine Lakes
Bristlecone-Glacier Trail

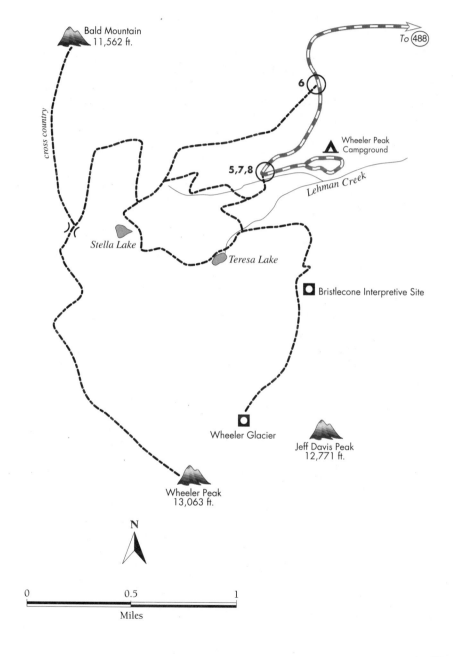

Bald Mountain
11,562 ft.

cross country

To (488)

6

5,7,8

Wheeler Peak
Campground

Lehman Creek

Stella Lake

Teresa Lake

Bristlecone Interpretive Site

Wheeler Glacier

Jeff Davis Peak
12,771 ft.

Wheeler Peak
13,063 ft.

N

0   0.5   1
Miles

7 Alpine Lakes

See Map on Page 45

Special attractions:	Alpine lakes and close-up views of the high peaks in the Snake Range.
Type of trail:	Loop.
Type of hike:	Day hike.
Total distance:	2.1 miles (3.4 km).
Difficulty:	Easy.
Elevation change:	From 10,000 to 10,400 feet (3,050 to 3,170 m).
Time required:	2 hours.
Water:	Stella Lake, Teresa Lake.
Maps:	USGS Windy Peak; Earthwalk Press Great Basin National Park.

Finding the trailhead: From Baker, drive west 5 miles (8 km) on the Great Basin National Park entrance road (Nevada Highway 488), then turn right (north) on the signed, paved Wheeler Peak Scenic Drive. Continue 12 miles (19.3 km) to the signed Bristlecone Trailhead, just before the road enters Wheeler Park Campground.

Key points in miles (km):

0.0 (0.0)	Trailhead.
0.2 (0.3)	Bristlecone-Glacier Trail; turn right.
0.7 (1.1)	Junction with Summit Trail; turn left.
0.8 (1.3)	Junction with Wheeler Peak Trail; stay left.
0.9 (1.5)	Stella Lake.
1.4 (2.3)	Teresa Lake.
1.6 (2.6)	Bristlecone-Glacier Trail; stay left.
1.9 (3.0)	Alpine Lakes Trail; stay right.
2.1 (3.4)	Trailhead.

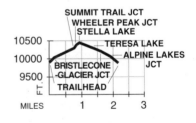

The hike: Although the Alpine Lakes Trail is relatively short, with little elevation gain, it lies at 10,000 feet above sea level. Most people, especially those who live near sea level, will have lowered hiking ability at this altitude. The signed trail crosses Lehman Creek on a small footbridge, then forks after a short distance. Turn right on the Alpine Lakes Trail, which climbs through Engelmann spruce–limber pine forest north of the creek. After crossing the creek again, the pleasant trail switchbacks to the right through meadows bordered with quaking aspen. Hikers get fine views of Wheeler Peak. Stay left at the signed junction with the Summit Trail. A short distance farther, the signed Wheeler Peak Trail turns sharply right; continue straight ahead to the first lake.

Stella Lake.

Wheeler Glacier.

Stella Lake is a typical glacial lake formed in the cirque created by a glacier. Moving glacial ice "ground down at the heel" and formed this depression in the floor of a steep-walled valley. After the ice melted, it left behind a deep, cold lake. Erosion of the steep mountainsides above the lake had gradually filled in the depression. Stella Lake is in the last stages of fill; it is shallow and freezes almost solid in winter.

The trail skirts Stella Lake on the left, then wanders through uneven, hummocky terrain. When the glacier that covered this area melted, it dropped its mixed load of dirt, sand, rocks, and boulders in a jumbled heap. Sometimes large blocks of ice are isolated from the retreating mass of a glacier, and later melt to form kettle lakes in depressions in the moraine. Several depressions along this section of the trail could contain small lakes, but don't. This is probably because of the present dryness of the climate.

The trail descends in a single switchback and follows a small stream to Teresa Lake. The depth of this lake varies greatly from year to year, depending on the amount of snowmelt. The trail skirts the lake on the left, then continues down the drainage. Just north of the lake, turn left at a signed junction with the Bristlecone-Glacier Trail. This trail can be done as a side trip; it adds 3.2 miles (5.1 km) to the length. (See Hike 8, Bristlecone-Glacier Trail, for details.) The trail continues north down the slope, and soon reaches the junction with the Alpine Lakes Trail where you started the loop. Stay right to reach the trailhead.

8   Bristlecone-Glacier Trail

See Map on Page 45

Special attractions:	Wheeler Glacier, which is the only permanent body of ice between the Sierra Nevada and the Wasatch Mountains, and a bristlecone pine interpretive trail visiting the oldest living trees on earth.
Type of trail:	Out and back.
Type of hike:	Day hike.
Total distance:	4.2 miles (6.8 km).
Difficulty:	Moderate.
Elevation change:	From 10,000 to 11,000 feet (3,048 to 3,350 m).
Water:	Teresa Lake.
Maps:	USGS Windy Peak; Earthwalk Press Great Basin National Park.

Finding the trailhead: From Baker, drive west 5 miles (8 km) on the Great Basin National Park entrance road (Nevada Highway 488), then turn right (north) on the signed, paved Wheeler Peak Scenic Drive. Continue 12 miles (19.3 km) to the signed Bristlecone Trailhead, just before the road enters Wheeler Peak Campground.

Key points in miles (km):

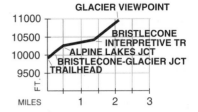

0.0	(0.0)	Trailhead.
0.2	(0.3)	Bristlecone-Glacier Trail; go left.
0.5	(0.8)	Alpine Lakes Trail; go left.
1.4	(2.3)	Bristlecone interpretive loop.
2.1	(3.4)	Glacier viewpoint.

The hike: From the trailhead, this moderate trail crosses Lehman Creek to reach a signed trail junction where hikers should turn left on the signed Bristlecone-Glacier Trail. The route climbs steadily through dense limber pine–Engelmann spruce forest, then meets the Alpine Lakes Trail at a signed junction. (See Hike 7 for details on the lakes.) Turn left (east) and follow the Bristlecone-Glacier Trail as it first crosses over a low ridge, then climbs across a shady, north-facing slope. Where the trail turns right at a ridge, there is a good view of the upper Lehman Creek drainage and the Wheeler Peak Campground.

Now the trail starts climbing gently along the slope. A switchback leads onto the rough, jumbled terrain of the moraine left by the retreat of Wheeler Glacier. A short, signed interpretive trail here explains the bristlecone pines. It is certainly worth the time and adds almost nothing to the hike's overall distance. Bristlecone pines are gnarled, tough trees found near timberline in the mountains of Colorado, Utah, Nevada, eastern California, and northern Arizona. They are easily recognized by their short, stiff needles growing five to a bundle and by their branches, which resemble neat bottle brushes. Bristlecones are among the oldest living things on Earth, reaching ages of greater than 4,500 years.

Researchers determine the ages of the trees using tree ring dating. A slender cylinder is screwed into the heart of the tree, a process that, if done correctly, leaves the tree unharmed. The cylinder is removed and the wood core extracted. Bands along the core are sections of the tree rings, and each ring represents a period of growth. Since bristlecones have one short period of growth each year, the rings may be counted and correlated with other tree ring data to determine the tree's age. The rings also indicate climate changes affecting the tree's growth rate. By correlating overlapping sections from older and dead trees in other places in the West, the tree ring record has been extended back 9,000 years.

After visiting the pines interpretive site, continue on the path. The two trails rejoin at a signed junction, and the Bristlecone-Glacier Trail continues up the moraine. The only trees that survive here are low mats of bristlecone pine, limber pine, and Engelmann spruce. In this stark canyon carved by ice and frost, life is reduced to a few hardy tundra plants growing in places where the rocks are stable: The trail ends at the foot of Wheeler Glacier. In late summer you may notice a red stain on the old snow; this is caused by an algae that is able to live on snowfields.

Glaciers form when the annual snowfall exceeds the amount of water lost to melting and evaporation. As the layers of snow pile up year after year, their weight compresses the lowest layers into ice. Under such great pressure, ice becomes fluid and begins to flow down the mountainside. The moving ice scours its bed, wearing away the bedrock and moving it downhill. The lower end of a glacier sits at the elevation where ice melts faster than it is replaced. Even a slight change in the climate can cause a rapid retreat or expansion of a glacier, so scientists study icefields worldwide as a sensitive indicator of climate change. When a glacier retreats, it drops its immense load of rock, forming a moraine, a distinctive heap of dirt, gravel, and rocks of all sizes.

9   Mountain View Nature Trail

Special attractions:	An easy interpretive trail explaining the piñon-juniper plant community and the geology of the Snake Range.
Type of trail:	Loop.
Type of trip:	Day hike.
Total distance:	0.5 mile (0.8 km).
Difficulty:	Easy.
Elevation change:	None. The trail is at 6,820 feet (2,080 m).
Time required:	1 hour.
Water:	Visitor center.
Maps:	A guide leaflet is available at the park visitor center.

Finding the trailhead: From Baker, drive west 5.6 miles (9 km) on Nevada Highway 488 and park at the Great Basin National Park Visitor Center.

The hike: This short nature trail is a good way to become familiar with the piñon-juniper plant community. It starts at the north end of the park visitor center, at the old log cabin. The cabin was a guest lodge during the early days of Lehman Cave National Monument. The trail continues behind the cabin, gradually climbing the slope until it reaches a viewpoint. Interpretive signs point out plants common in the Great Basin.

10 Lehman Cave

Special attractions: An easy walk through Lehman Cave.
Type of trail: Loop.
Type of trip: Ranger-guided cave walk.
Total distance: 0.6 mile (1 km).
Difficulty: Easy.
Elevation change: Little. The cave mouth is at 6,820 feet (2,080 m).
Time required: 1 to 1.5 hours.
Water: None.
Maps: Lehman Cave park brochure.

Finding the trailhead: From Baker, drive west 5.6 miles (9 km) on Nevada Highway 488 and park at the Great Basin National Park Visitor Center.

The hike: Though small compared to famous caves such as Carlsbad Caverns, Lehman Cave is highly decorated with natural cave formations and is well worth a visit. To protect the cave's resources, park rangers lead guided walks through its caverns. Check at the park visitor center for walk times, fees, and advance ticket sales. Groups are limited to 30. Some cave passages are narrow, so camera tripods and backpacks are not allowed. Sections of the trail through the cave may be wet and slippery, and the path ascends and descends several sets of stairs.

11 Baker and Johnson Lakes

Special attractions: Scenic hike to a pair of alpine lakes.
Type of trail: Loop.
Type of trip: Long day hike or overnight backpack trip.
Total distance: 11.2 miles (18 km).
Difficulty: Difficult.
Elevation change: From 8,000 to 11,300 feet (3,440 to 3,445 m).
Time required: 10 hours.
Water: Baker Creek, Baker Lake, Johnson Lake, South Fork Baker Creek.
Maps: USGS Wheeler Peak, Kious Spring; Earthwalk Press Great Basin National Park.

Finding the trailhead: From Baker, drive west 5.2 miles (8.4 km) on Nevada Highway 488, the entrance road to Great Basin National Park. Just after passing the park boundary sign, turn left (south) on the signed, maintained dirt Baker Creek Road. Follow this road 4 miles (6.5 km) to its end at the signed Baker Trailhead.

Key points in miles (km):

- 0.0 (0.0)   Trailhead.
- 3.5 (5.6)   Old cabin.
- 3.9 (6.3)   Junction with Baker–Johnson Trail.
- 4.7 (7.6)   Baker Lake.
- 4.8 (7.7)   Cross-country route to Baker–Johnson Trail.
- 5.0 (8.0)   Baker–Johnson Trail; turn right.
- 5.6 (9.0)   Johnson pass.
- 6.0 (9.7)   Johnson Lake.
- 7.4 (11.9) Junction with trail to Snake–Baker Pass; turn left.
- 8.0 (12.9) Snake–Baker Pass.
- 8.5 (13.7) Junction with South Fork Baker Creek Trail; turn left.
- 11.1 (17.8) Junction with Timber Creek Trail; turn left.
- 11.2 (18.0) Trailhead.

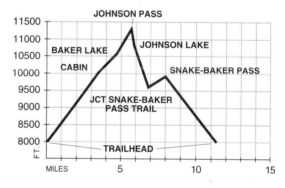

The hike: Start on the signed Baker Lake Trail. The trail climbs along the north side of boisterous Baker Creek, sometimes swinging north in a series of switchbacks. Hikers get varied views of the canyon walls and the high country, especially when the trail temporarily leaves the creek and its dense riparian vegetation. Other sections of trail stay near the creek in fine aspen groves.

After a long climb, the trail passes the ruins of an old cabin. It was probably used by Peter Deishman, a prospector who mined actively here in the early part of the twentieth century. Beyond the cabin, continue on the main trail, which climbs the steep slope below Baker Lake in a series of switchbacks. Watch for a faint, unsigned trail (leading to Johnson Pass) going left, but stay on the main trail (right) and continue to Baker Lake. This small, scenic alpine lake is set amid the rugged cliffs of the Snake Range crest and Baker Peak.

After enjoying the lake, start back down the trail, but watch for a cairned cross-country route going right (southeast) before the main trail starts its steep descent. Follow the cairns as they contour southeast a short distance to join the faint Baker–Johnson trail in the open valley above timberline. If you don't find the trail along the creek, just follow the drainage and the cairns uphill. The route reaches broad Johnson Pass at 11,294 feet (3,442 m). Enjoy the sweeping views, including Baker Peak, Jeff Davis Peak, and, close at hand, Pyramid Peak. When you are ready to head down, look for a few cairns and use them to descend south from the pass. The trail becomes well defined on the steep slope below you. Early season hikers will have to avoid one or more steep snowfields. If the trail is lost under snow, pick it up farther downslope.

Old cabin along the Baker Lake Trail.

Baker and Johnson Lakes • Timber Creek–South Fork Baker Creek • Johnson Lake • Dead Lake Snake Creek

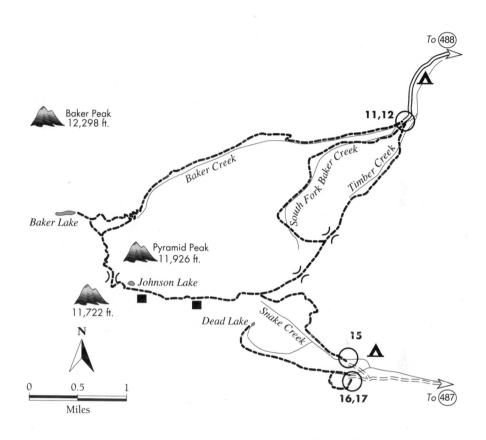

The trail soon joins a much better (but still little-used) trail that goes right (southwest) to the old Johnson tungsten mine, established by Alfred Johnson in the fall of 1909. Turn left here, going downhill, and continue to the south shore of Johnson Lake. You will pass more relics of the old mine, including an aerial tram cable spanning the talus slope below the mine entry. Timbers and other old mining gear are scattered along the east shore of the lake, apparently brought down by a major snow avalanche in 1935. This event destroyed most of the mine workings and put an end to an already marginal venture.

The trail, now an old jeep road, continues down the drainage east of the lake and gradually becomes more distinct. Watch for the ruins of several old cabins used by workers for the mining operation. Good camping spots dot this area, and water is available in the creek. The trail descends steeply after leaving the cabins. About a mile below Johnson Lake, it passes the ruins of a large log structure, the old Johnson mill. Ore was brought down to Johnson Lake via the aerial tram, then transported on mules to the mill. Once the tungsten ore was concentrated, mules carried it on down the mountain and eventually to the railhead at Frisco, Utah. Transportation costs were high, which probably contributed to the closure of the mine.

Look for more campsites in the forest below the mill, on the south side of the trail. If you choose to stay at these dry sites, you will have to carry water down from the creek. About 0.3 mile (0.5 km) beyond the mill site, you will pass an old road closure gate. This is the signal to start watching for the signed trail to Snake-Baker Pass. The foot trail is little used and easy to miss. It climbs steadily through aspens to reach the pass, where the trail becomes faint. Turn left (north), and descend the trail below the pass, northeast through the forest.

Shortly, the trail emerges into a broad meadow. A wide pass is visible above to the right. Follow the trail, faint now, across the meadow toward this pass. Just as it starts to climb, a sign points out the South Fork Baker Creek Trail to the left, and Timber Creek Trail ahead, over the pass. Turn left (west) and descend into the South Fork. (Note: This junction is shown incorrectly on the USGS map.) Pick up the trail again as it nears the right side of the creek where it enters the trees. From the junction, it is about 2.6 miles (4.2 km) to a signed junction with the Timber Creek Trail. At that point turn left. The trail crosses three bridges on Baker Creek before it reaches the Baker Trailhead.

Baker Lake.

12 Timber Creek–South Fork Baker Creek

See Map on Page 55

Special attractions:	A little-used trail to a high pass and scenic alpine meadows.
Type of trail:	Loop.
Type of trip:	Day hike or overnight backpack trip.
Total distance:	4.7 miles (7.7 km).
Difficulty:	Moderate.
Elevation change:	From 8,000 to 9,640 feet (2,440 to 2,940 m).
Time required:	4 hours.
Water:	Timber Creek, South Fork Baker Creek.
Maps:	USGS Wheeler Peak, Kious Spring; Earthwalk Press Great Basin National Park.

Finding the trailhead: From Baker, drive west 5.2 miles (8.4 km) on Nevada Highway 488, the entrance road to Great Basin National Park. Just after passing the park boundary sign, turn left (south) on the signed, maintained dirt Baker Creek Road. Follow this road 4 miles (6.5 km) to its end at the signed Baker Trailhead.

Key points in miles (km):

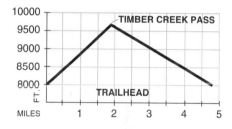

0.0 (0.0)	Trailhead.
0.1 (0.2)	Timber Creek Trail junction; turn left.
1.9 (3.1)	Timber Creek pass.
2.0 (3.2)	South Fork Baker Creek Trail junction; turn right.
4.6 (7.4)	Timber Creek Trail junction; turn left.
4.7 (7.7)	Trailhead.

The hike: Two trails leave the Baker Trailhead. Take the left trail, signed Johnson Lake. Cross Baker Creek on a couple of footbridges, then watch for the signed junction with the Timber Creek Trail. Here, go left (south), and follow the sometimes faint trail as it crosses a meadow into Timber Creek Canyon. The trail begins to climb steeply, and continues through a beautiful fir and aspen forest. A set of log steps marks the point where the climb starts to relent, and soon afterward the trail comes out onto a wide sage-covered saddle framed by aspens.

Cross the saddle and descend west into the head of South Fork Baker Creek. There are great views of the east side of Pyramid Peak. The trail is faint across the meadow, so just head down into the South Fork. The trail becomes obvious again as it enters the aspens, following the right (east) side of the creek. The South Fork trail is better maintained than the Timber Creek Trail. It is also slightly longer, so the descent is more gradual. A steeper

A view of Pyramid Peak from the South Fork Baker Creek Trail.

descent in the lower part of the canyon leads to the junction with the Timber Creek Trail; turn left (northeast) here, and cross the two footbridges on your way back to the trailhead.

13 Pole Canyon

Special attractions:	A little-used trail at low elevation, good for early season hikes.
Type of trail:	Out and back.
Type of trip:	Day hike.
Total distance:	4.2 miles (6.7 km)
Difficulty:	Moderate.
Elevation change:	From 6,820 to 7,760 feet (2,080 to 2,365 m).
Time required:	4 hours.
Water:	Pole Creek.
Maps:	USGS Kious Spring

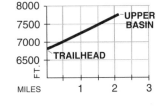

Finding the trailhead: From Baker, drive west 5.2 miles (8.4 km) on Nevada Highway 488, the entrance road to the park. Just after passing the park boundary sign, turn left (south) on the signed, maintained dirt Baker Creek Road. Follow this road 1.6 miles (2.6 km), then turn left on the Gray Cliffs Road, which also has a maintained dirt surface. Almost immediately, turn left again on an unmaintained road. Go 0.6 mile (1 km). Just past a cattleguard,

Pole Canyon • Can Young Canyon

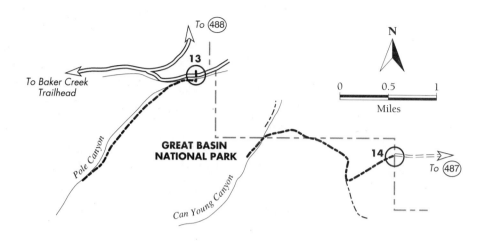

look for an unsigned trailhead on the right. Begin here. The trail is an old, closed jeep road that immediately crosses Baker Creek.

Key points in miles (km):

0.0 (0.0)   Trailhead.
2.1 (3.4)   Upper basin.

The hike: Due to its relatively low elevation, this is a good hike for early season when the high country is still snow covered. It is also great in fall, when the aspens are changing color. The old jeep road crosses Baker Creek, which you will probably have to wade. Use caution as you do so. In spring or after heavy rain, the creek can be too high to cross safely.

On the far side of the creek, the trail turns right and follows the left side of the stream through open piñon-juniper country. Soon the loud rush of Baker Creek fades, replaced by the gentle murmur of Pole Creek, a much smaller stream. The old road enters groves of aspen and becomes criss-crossed with deadfall. Persistence will pay off. Just as the deadfall is getting really annoying, the trail climbs out of the streamcourse on the left side and skirts a sage-covered slope. It passes though an aspen grove at about 7,600 feet (2,300 m), and emerges into the upper basin of Pole Canyon. The trail fades away here, though with care it could probably be followed to the spring shown on the topographic map. But the basin itself makes an excellent destination for the hike, with scenic views all around.

Rock buttress and pinyon pine, along the route to Can Young Canyon.

14 Can Young Canyon

See Map on Page 59

Special attractions:	An easy, low elevation hike that's a good choice early in the spring.
Type of trail:	Out and back.
Type of trip:	Day hike.
Total distance:	4.8 miles (7.7 km).
Difficulty:	Easy.
Elevation change:	From 6,480 to 7,200 feet (1,975 to 2,195 m).
Time required:	3 hours.
Water:	Can Young Canyon.
Maps:	USGS Kious Spring; Earthwalk Press Great Basin National Park; Humboldt National Forest–Ely Ranger District.

Finding the trailhead: From Baker, drive 1 mile (1.6 km) southeast on Nevada Highway 487, then turn right on a maintained dirt road. The road goes past a large water tank. At 2.4 miles (3.9 km) from the highway, turn right onto an unmaintained road, which requires a high-clearance vehicle. Go right at a minor fork in another 0.3 mile (0.5 km), and continue to the Great Basin National Park boundary at 3.5 miles (5.6 km) from the highway. Park here, since the road becomes much rougher ahead.

Key points in miles (km):
- 0.0 (0.0)   Trailhead at the park boundary.
- 0.7 (1.1)   T junction at water trough; turn right.
- 1.1 (1.8)   Junction below saddle; stay left.
- 2.1 (3.4)   Can Young Canyon; turn left.
- 2.4 (3.9)   End of hike.

The hike: This is a good route early in the hiking season, before the snow has melted from the high country. Walk up the road from the park boundary. The road appears to be used only occasionally, so it makes a nice hike. will have a good view of impressive cliffs to the left of the road.

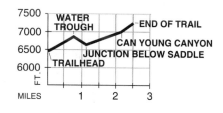

The road reaches a T intersection at a cattle watering trough in Kious Basin. Turn right, downhill, and follow the old road as it swings around another impressive cliff. Where a road forks right, go left and uphill, to the northwest. Within a few yards the road you are following mounts a saddle formed by a large rock knob. Beyond the saddle, the road goes through a gate, temporarily leaving the park. After this, the road climbs slowly along the foothills, then climbs more steeply into the mouth of Can Young Canyon.

Cross the flowing creek in the canyon bottom, then, at another T intersection, turn left and walk past the park boundary sign into the canyon. The road is closed to vehicles at this point. The old road continues along the creek, past fine aspen stands, before fading and becoming blocked by deadfall. This makes a good turnaround point.

15 Johnson Lake

See Map on Page 55

Special attractions:	A little-used trail to an alpine lake and historic mining district.
Type of trail:	Out and back.
Type of trip:	Day hike or backpack trip.
Total distance:	6.8 miles (10.9 km).
Difficulty:	Difficult.
Elevation change:	From 8,320 to 10,760 feet (2,535 to 3,280 m).
Time required:	7 hours.
Water:	Snake Creek, Johnson Lake.
Maps:	USGS Wheeler Peak; Earthwalk Press Great Basin National Park.

Finding the trailhead: From Baker, drive south 5.2 miles (8.4 km) on Nevada Highway 487, then turn right (west) on the signed, graded Snake Creek Canyon Road. Follow this road 13 miles (20.9 km) to its end. You will pass numerous primitive campsites. Just before the end of the road, a jeep road goes left; stay on the main road. The trailhead has a primitive campground with picnic tables in a fine aspen grove surrounding Snake Creek.

Key points in miles (km):
- 0.0 (0.0) Trailhead.
- 2.0 (3.2) Trail to Snake-Baker Pass; stay left.
- 3.4 (5.5) Johnson Lake.

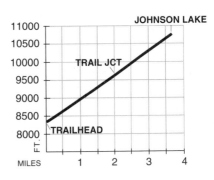

The hike: The Johnson Lake Trail follows an old jeep trail that is closed to vehicles. It is not marked or maintained, so you should carry a topographic map. Start from the upper end of the parking lot and follow the unsigned old road directly up the hill. After a few hundred yards another jeep road comes in from the left. Here, your trail turns right and crosses Snake Creek. It stays north of Snake Creek all the way to Johnson Lake. After crossing the creek, the trail parallels the watercourse on the right, climbing through alpine meadows bordered with aspen and white fir.

Pyramid Peak.

Forest typical to the Snake Range is well represented along the Johnson Lake Trail. Great Basin trees such as curlleaf mountain mahogany grow next to Rocky Mountain white fir and Engelmann spruce. Douglas-fir is also common, as is limber pine. Along this section of the trail you can identify white fir by its flat needles, which will not roll in your fingers, and its spongy, corklike bark. Douglas-fir needles are similar, but Douglas-fir bark is gray and more deeply furrowed. Limber pine has 2-inch needles growing five to a bunch, and its limbs are very flexible, helping the tree to survive heavy alpine snow loads.

After following the creek for a while, the trail veers north and descends to cross a drainage. It then climbs onto a sage-covered slope, which it ascends in a couple of switchbacks. Notice the contrast between this dry south-facing slope, covered with sage and mountain mahogany, and the moist north-facing slope you just descended, covered with fir and aspen. Above the switchbacks, the trail climbs steeply through forest in which limber pines start to appear. You will also see Engelmann spruce. Its needles grow singly like those of the firs, but are square in cross-section so that they roll easily between your fingers.

You may notice a faint, unsigned trail going right. This trail climbs to Snake–Baker Pass; if you see it, stay left on the Johnson Lake Trail. The trail now heads off a minor forest drainage and climbs onto a point. Here, the forest takes on a decidedly more alpine appearance. Campsites are plentiful here, but have no water after the snow melts. In another half mile, the trail passes an old cabin. There are a few campsites here, too, and there is water in the creek. Be sure to camp at least 100 feet from the water.

After leaving the cabin, the old road becomes rougher and steeper for about 0.5 mile (0.9 km), then moderates a bit for the final climb to Johnson Lake. More cabins, one of them fairly elaborate, are located just below the lake. Various cut logs and rusty pieces of equipment have been strewn around

Snake Creek near Dead Lake.

the cabins and lake, indicating a great deal of activity once took place here. Above, a cable is strung from one of the mines high on the talus slope. Some of the cut timber at the lakeshore might have been used to support a tramway. The lake itself is small, but its west end is deep. It is a true alpine tarn—a lake created by a glacier.

16 Dead Lake

See Map on Page 55

Special attractions:	An alpine creek and meadows in a seldom-visited area; optional loop hike.
Type of trail:	Out and back.
Type of trip:	Day hike or easy backpack trip.
Total distance:	3.2 miles (5.1 km); the optional loop is 4.2 miles (6.8 km).
Difficulty:	Moderate.
Elevation change:	From 8,240 to 9,600 feet (2,510 to 2,925 m).
Time required:	3 hours.
Water:	Snake Creek.
Maps:	USGS Wheeler Peak; Earthwalk Press Great Basin National Park.

Finding the trailhead: From Baker, drive south 5.2 miles (8.4 km) on Nevada Highway 487, then turn right (west) on the signed, graded Snake Creek Canyon Road. After 13 miles (20.9 km), the main road veers right, away from Snake Creek. Turn left on a faint, unmaintained road. Ignore the first left fork; take the second left and park at the unsigned trailhead. If you miss the turnoff, you will reach Shoshone Campground at the end of the main road. From there, backtrack the short distance to the unmaintained road.

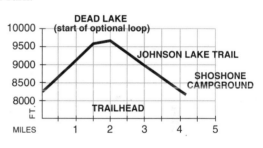

Key points in miles (km):
   0.0 (0.0)   Trailhead on the unmaintained road.
   1.6 (2.6)   Dead Lake; start of optional loop hike.
   2.0 (3.2)   Johnson Lake Trail; turn right.
   4.0 (6.4)   Shoshone Campground.
   4.2 (6.8)   Trailhead.

The hike: Walk up the old road on which you were just driving. You will soon pass the limit of vehicle use, where the road starts to climb steadily. As piñon-juniper and ponderosa pine give way to fir and aspen, hikers get occasional great views to the east. Just beyond where the old jeep trail swings right, watch for a foot trail branching to the right. A short, steep climb on this trail leads to a flat bench where the central fork of Snake Creek flows through small alpine meadows. Dead Lake is about 300 yards (300 m) farther northeast.

Hikers who carry the USGS map and are familiar with cross-country hiking can make a nice loop. From the lake, contour north, cross-country, through the alpine forest. After about 0.6 mile (1 km), you will meet the Johnson Lake Trail, an old jeep road. Turn right and follow this good trail 2 miles (3.2 km) downhill to Shoshone Campground. To return to your trailhead, walk down the main road to the faint road at Snake Creek, then turn right and walk uphill a short distance to your car.

17 Snake Creek

See Map on Page 55

Special attractions:	An easy day hike along Snake Creek.
Type of trail:	Loop.
Type of trip:	Day hike.
Total distance:	0.8 mile (1.3 km).
Difficulty:	Easy.
Elevation change:	From 8,240 to 8,400 feet (2,510 to 2,560 m).
Time required:	1 hour.
Water:	Snake Creek.
Maps:	USGS Wheeler Peak.

Finding the trailhead: From Baker, drive south 5.2 miles (8.4 km) on Nevada Highway 487, then turn right (west) on the signed, graded Snake Creek Canyon Road. After 13 miles (20.9 km), the main road veers right, away from Snake Creek. Turn left on a faint, unmaintained road. Take the first left turn, cross the creek, and park in the primitive campsite.

Key points in miles (km):
    0.0 (0.0)   Trailhead at primitive campsite.
    0.5 (0.8)   End of old road.
    0.6 (1.0)   Dead Lake Trail.
    0.8 (1.3)   Trailhead.

The hike: This short trail is worthwhile because it takes you to a tributary of Snake Creek. Cross the campground and follow the old road that climbs left (northeast) out of the camp area. Several switchbacks lead to the road's abrupt end. Now turn right and drop directly downhill, cross-country, to the creek. Cross the creek, then turn right on the Dead Lake Trail, an old road, and follow it back to the trailhead. Or just follow the creek downhill to the trailhead.

18 South Fork Big Wash

See Map on Page 71

Special attractions: A seldom-used trail in a remote section of the park.
Type of trail: Out and back.
Type of trip: Day hike or backpack trip.
Total distance: 8.4 miles (13.5 km).
Difficulty: Moderate.
Elevation change: From 8,030 to 6,760 feet (2,445 to 2,060 m).
Time required: 7 hours.
Water: Springs at old boiler, along traverse above gorge, and at end of hike.
Maps: USGS Arch Canyon,Kious Spring; Earthwalk Press Great Basin National Park.

Finding the trailhead: From Baker, drive southeast 10.7 miles (17.2 km) on Nevada Highway 487; the road becomes Utah Highway 21 at the state line. Turn right on the first dirt road past Pruess Lake (signed Lexington Arch). Go west 9.6 miles (15.4 km), then turn right at a fork where the left branch leads to Lexington Arch. You may want a high-clearance vehicle, though most cars should be able to continue to the trailhead, if driven with care. Continue 3.8 miles (6.1 km) to reach the unsigned trailhead. The trail is the old jeep road on the right (north).

Key points in miles (km):

0.0 (0.0) Trailhead at old jeep road.
0.4 (0.6) Park boundary.
1.3 (2.1) Sawmill site in South Fork Big Wash.
3.0 (4.8) Trail returns to South Fork Big Wash.
3.7 (5.9) Park boundary.
4.2 (6.8) North Fork Big Wash.

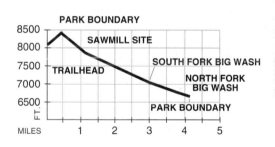

The hike: The old jeep road climbs steeply to a broad saddle and enters Great Basin National Park at a signed gate. It then descends through fir-aspen forest, switches back sharply to the right (northeast), and descends to the dry bed of South Fork Big Wash. The remains of an old steam boiler from a defunct sawmill sit near the wash bottom. The trail continues as a footpath, climbing out of the wash on the left (north) slope. This section of trail is faint, but the path soon becomes easy to follow.

The trail next goes around a juniper and crosses the flow from a spring. It climbs through dense stands of mountain mahogany, with occasional tantalizing glimpses of the narrow limestone gorge below. After leveling off, the trail passes another spring, then continues around the slope to the north. An open section of ponderosa pine and manzanita affords a great view down South Fork Big Wash.

67

South fork, Snake Creek.

After rounding a broad basin, the trail turns east and begins to descend rapidly. It reaches the creekbed below Castle Butte, a prominent limestone cliff, then crosses to the south side. Below this point, a fine spring enters from the north, and the creek runs steadily. The trail then goes through a narrow slot in the limestone, made narrower still by a huge fallen boulder. This marks the approximate park boundary. The canyon opens into a broad flat at the confluence of North Fork Big Wash, the turnaround point of your hike.

19 Lexington Arch

Special attractions: A unique limestone natural arch.
Type of trail: Out and back.
Type of trip: Day hike.
Total distance: 3 miles (4.8 km).
Difficulty: Moderate.
Elevation change: From 7,440 to 8,440 feet (2,270 to 2,570 m).
Time required: 3 hours.
Water: None.
Maps: USGS Arch Canyon; Earthwalk Press Great Basin National Park; Humboldt National Forest–Ely Ranger District.

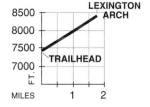

Finding the trailhead: From Baker, drive southeast 10.7 miles (17.2 km) on Nevada Highway 487, which becomes Utah Highway 21 at the state line. Turn right on the first dirt road past Pruess Lake (signed Lexington Arch). Go west 11.7 miles (18.8 km), following the signs. This road is minimally maintained, so a high-clearance vehicle is recommended. Please leave all gates as you find them to help keep livestock on the correct ranges.

Old steam boiler, South Fork Big Wash.

Lexington Arch.

Key points in miles (km):
  0.0 (0.0)   Trailhead.
  1.5 (2.4)   Lexington Arch.

The hike: The trail to Lexington Arch at first follows the Big Wash drainage, but after about 200 yards it turns left and climbs the sage slope to the west in a series of broad switchbacks. It then traverses the forested south slopes of the canyon. The trail returns to the bed of the canyon at the south buttress of the arch and, finally, climbs into the arch itself.

Rising high above the floor of the canyon, this imposing natural arch was created by the forces of weather over a span of centuries. Lexington Arch is unusual in one important aspect: it is carved from limestone, when most natural arches in the western United States are composed of sandstone. Geologists speculate that the arch was once a passage in a cave system. Flowstone, a smooth, glossy deposit that forms in caves, has been found at the base of the arch opening, lending support to this theory. Some suggest that Lexington "Arch" is actually a natural bridge. An arch is formed by the forces of weathering, such as ice, wind, and chemical breakdown of the rock. A natural bridge, in contrast, is formed by the flowing waters of a stream. It is possible that long ago, when the canyon was less deep, the waters of Lexington Creek flowed through a cave in the canyon wall, enlarging it to what later became Lexington Arch.

South Fork Big Wash • Lexington Arch

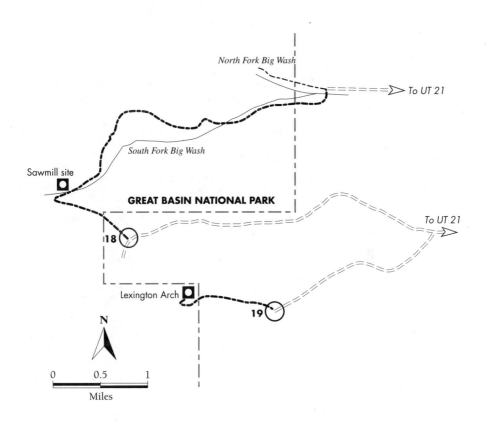

North Fork Big Wash

To UT 21

South Fork Big Wash

Sawmill site

GREAT BASIN NATIONAL PARK

To UT 21

18

19

Lexington Arch

N

0   0.5   1
Miles

Pinyon pine and cliffs along Smith Creek.

Mount Moriah Wilderness

20 Smith Creek

Special attractions:	A remote canyon with limestone caves and cliffs.
Type of trail:	Out and back.
Type of trip:	Day hike.
Total distance:	4.2 miles (6.8 km).
Difficulty:	Moderate.
Elevation change:	From 5,880 to 6,440 feet (1,790 to 1,960 m).
Time required:	4 hours.
Water:	Smith Creek.
Maps:	USGS Mount Moriah, Little Horse Canyon; Humboldt National Forest–Ely Ranger District.

Finding the trailhead: From Baker, drive 5 miles (8 km) northwest on Nevada Highway 487, then turn right (east) on U.S. Highway 6/50. Almost immediately, take the next left (northeast); the correct road passes a small electrical substation. Stay on this road, going northeast through the Snake Valley. After a couple of

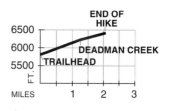

miles, the surface becomes maintained dirt. Continue for 10.9 miles (17.4 km) to a crossroads. Go straight ahead on the main road to reach a small ranch at 26.9 miles (43.3 km) from US 6/50, then turn left on the signed ·Smith Creek Road. Follow this minimally maintained dirt road 7.1 miles (11.4 km) to its end. There are a couple of rough creek crossings near the end of the road, and their condition changes from year to year. If necessary, park and walk to the trailhead at road's end. This is the Mount Moriah Wilderness boundary. Smith Creek has water, and there is limited camping (with shade) at a small site 100 yards before the trailhead.

Key points in miles (km):
0.0 (0.0)   Trailhead.
1.3 (2.1)   Deadman Creek.
2.1 (3.4)   Trail fades out.

The hike: The unsigned trail up Smith Creek gets very little use. It starts as an old jeep trail and climbs away from the creek on the north, giving great views of the impressive canyon. It then crosses the creek and enters a cot-

Smith Creek

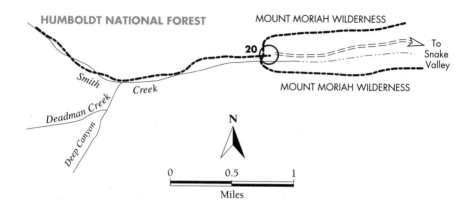

tonwood grove. Deadman Creek enters noisily from the left (south), pouring over a series of ledges. Continue up Smith Creek on the now much fainter trail.

Since it was built as a jeep road, the trail always crosses the creek when the bench peters out. The canyon gradually narrows, and the high cliff on the north side becomes especially impressive. Hikers also get tantalizing views of the high country, far above to the south.

About 2.1 miles (3.4 km) from the trailhead, the old trail drops into the bed of the creek and fades out. Our hike ends here, but experienced hikers can continue to Ryegrass Canyon by following the best route on their topographic map. Other exploration possibilities are Deadman Creek and its several tributaries.

21 Hendrys Creek

Special attractions:	Access to The Table and Mount Moriah via a scenic canyon with a good trail.
Type of trail:	Out and back.
Type of trip:	Two- or three-day backpack trip.
Total distance:	19.8 miles (31.9 km).
Difficulty:	Difficult.
Elevation change:	From 5,900 to 11,000 feet (1,800 to 3,350 m).
Time required:	16 hours.
Water:	Hendrys Creek.
Maps:	USGS The Cove, Old Mans Canyon, and Mount Moriah; Humboldt National Forest–Ely Ranger District.

Finding the trailhead: From Baker, drive 5 miles (8 km) northwest on Nevada Highway 487, then turn right (east) on U.S. Highway 6/50. Almost immediately, take the next left (northeast). The correct road passes a small electrical substation. Stay on this road northeast through the Snake Valley; the surface becomes maintained dirt after a couple of miles. Continue for 10.9 miles (17.5 km) to a crossroads. Turn left (northwest) on the signed, maintained dirt road to Hendrys Creek and the Hatch Rock mining operation. Take this road 3 miles (4.8 km), then turn left at a sign for the Hendrys Creek trailhead. Go another 0.1 mile (0.2 km), then turn right at an unsigned junction. After 0.3 mile (0.5 km), turn left at another sign for the trailhead. In another 0.6 mile (1 km), you will pass the national forest boundary and reach the signed trailhead. There is neither shade nor good camping at the trailhead.

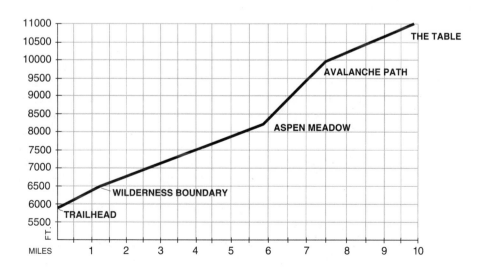

Hendrys Creek • Big Canyon Trail

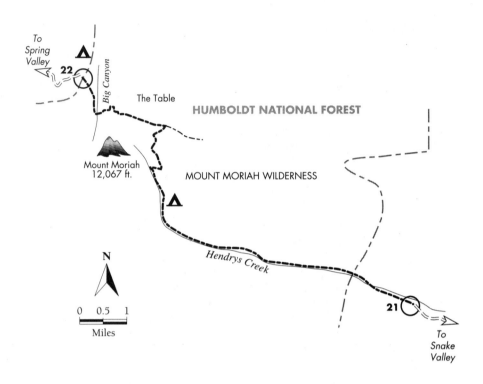

Key points in miles (km):
0.0 (0.0)   Trailhead.
1.5 (2.4)   Wilderness boundary.
5.9 (9.5)   Aspen meadow.
7.5 (10.5) Avalanche path.
9.9 (15.9) The Table.

The hike: The well-maintained Hendrys Creek Trail starts along the south side of the creek but soon crosses north to follow an old jeep road. Surrounding hillsides hold sagebrush and grass, but the streamcourse is dense with willow and cottonwood, plus a few stately ponderosa pines. Watch for occasional poison ivy along the first mile. As the trail gradually climbs, ponderosa pine becomes more common, almost dominant for a while. Within a mile of the trailhead, there's plenty of shade along the trail. The dramatic canyon walls, covered with piñon and juniper, start to close in. You will pass the signed wilderness boundary at about 1.5 miles (2.4 km). The creek runs nicely along your route, and the lower section of the canyon has plenty of camping for those who only want to walk a mile or two.

After about 2 miles (3.2 km), quaking aspen start to appear, and the canyon walls become more forested. Hendrys Creek has been a popular place for many years, as the multitude of inscriptions on the aspen show. At about 9,000 feet above sea level, 5.9 miles (9.5 km) from the trailhead, the trail enters an aspen-bordered meadow that offers a glimpse of Mount Moriah high to the northwest. There are several possible campsites here. This would be a good destination for the first day of a two- or three-day trip. The Table and Mount Moriah are within easy reach.

The good trail continues up Hendrys Creek, climbing more steeply now. At about 10,000 feet in elevation and 7.5 miles (10.5 km) from the start of your trek, the trail enters another, steeper meadow that offers even better views. This meadow is apparently the lower end of several large avalanche paths that start on Moriah's east face. The trail switchbacks to the east, leaving the meadow, then climbs a gentle ridge through open forest. After crossing a couple of canyons on the northeast slopes of Mount Moriah, it climbs a final slope to the south rim of The Table.

This 11,000-foot plateau slopes gently to the north. It is an arctic plain, open and treeless, but not lifeless—during the short growing season alpine flowers such as phlox and blue columbine manage to flower here. The south edge of The Table is bordered with twisted, picturesque bristlecone pines. By walking a short distance north, hikers can view most of the surrounding ranges, including Jeff Davis and Wheeler peaks in the south Snake Range. Unlike most high mountain viewpoints in Nevada, this one doesn't offer a view of the surrounding canyons and ridges. The high rim of The Table blocks the nearer view, making this vantage point seem especially remote.

A sign points back down Hendrys Creek and marks the junction with two cairned trails; the trail to Big Creek is on the west, and the route to

The Table.

Hampton and Horse creeks is on the east. These other trails suggest the possibility of a traverse across the range using a car shuttle. Be warned, however, that most trails shown on the Forest Service and USGS maps for this area are little used, faint, and difficult to find. Most of the Mount Moriah Wilderness should be considered cross-country hiking, requiring experience with a map and a compass. Those who have the skills and equipment will find a lot of wild country to explore.

22 Big Canyon Trail

See Map on Page 76

Special attractions: Easy access to The Table and Mount Moriah from a high trailhead reached via a scenic road.

Type of trail: Out and back.

Type of trip: Day hike.

Total distance: 6.2 miles (10 km).

Difficulty: Moderate.

Elevation change: From 9,900 to 11,000 feet (3,020 to 3,350 m).

Time required: 4 hours.

Water: Spring in Big Canyon.

Maps: USGS Sixmile Canyon, Mount Moriah; Humboldt National Forest–Ely Ranger District.

Finding the trailhead: From Baker, drive 5 miles (8 km) northwest on Nevada Highway 487, then turn left (west) on U.S. Highway 6/50. Continue 14.4 miles (23.2 km), crossing Sacramento Pass, then turn right on a maintained dirt road. This road starts westward but then turns north along the east side of the Spring Valley. Follow it for 12.1 miles

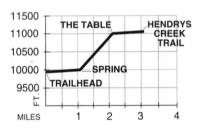

(19.5 km), then turn right (east) onto Fourmile Road, an unmaintained dirt road (Forest Road 469) just before crossing a cattleguard. Drive east 2.6 miles (4.2 km) to the foothills, then bear left. The road crosses a drainage, then climbs to a small saddle and a cattleguard after 0.3 mile (0.5 km).

To continue beyond this point, you will probably need a high-clearance, four-wheel-drive vehicle. The road beyond climbs steeply up a scenic ridge, gaining 2,000 feet in 3 miles (4.8 km). At the top of the climb, several minor roads branch left; stay right on the main road. After another 3.2 miles (5.2 km), a minor road turns left; go straight on the main road. In 0.1 mile (0.2 km), you will pass a small Forest Service cabin on the right in a stand of aspen. The cabin is open to the public and makes a good emergency shelter;

Bristlecone Pines on The Table.

please leave it as you found it. Continue 1.9 miles (3.1 km), crossing Deadman Creek, to the signed trailhead at the end of the road. There is a small campsite just north of the trailhead.

Key points in miles (km):
0.0 (0.0)	Trailhead.
1.1 (1.8)	Spring where trail starts to climb out of Big Canyon.
2.1 (3.4)	The Table.
3.1 (5.0)	Junction with Hendrys Creek Trail.

The hike: This hike is worth it just for the view from the trailhead. As you start the walk south into Big Canyon, the rugged northwest face of Mount Moriah is framed in the canyon before you. The trail drops gradually into the bottom of Big Canyon, then follows the bed upstream through aspen, fir, and limber pine forest. Big Canyon is normally dry, but there is a small, unnamed spring (not shown on the topographic map) next to the trail just after it turns sharply left and starts to climb the canyon's east slopes. This steep, switchbacking section lasts for about a mile until the trail reaches the southwest rim of The Table.

Continue east as the trail skirts the north ridge of Mount Moriah. At first, The Table is graced with a fine stand of gnarled, timberline bristlecone pine, but it soon becomes a treeless, arctic plateau. After walking across the plateau for a mile, you will reach a cairn marking the junction with the Hendrys Creek Trail, which drops south into Hendrys Creek.

With such an easy approach trail, you should have plenty of time to explore The Table. Mount Moriah is an easy, 1,000-foot (300-m) climb from anywhere along the last mile of this hike. Another great hike is to go out to the north edge of The Table, a walk of about 1 mile (1.6 km) one way. More bristlecone groves skirt the north edge of the plateau, where the view into Deadman Creek and the other tributaries of Smith Creek is excellent. With a car shuttle, you could use the Hendrys Creek Trail to do a two- or three-day backpack trip traversing the range. The Hampton and Horse Creek trails on the east side of the range could also be used for extended trips.

Appendix A—Resources

U.S. Bureau of Land Management—Nevada State Office
850 Harvard Way
P.O. Box 12000
Reno, NV 89520
702-785-6400

U.S. Bureau of Land Management—Ely District Office
702 N. Industrial Way
Ely, NV 89301
702-289-1800

Appendix B—Further Reading

Fletcher, Colin. *The Complete Walker III*. New York: Alfred A. Knopf, 1989.

Kricher, John C., and Gordon Morrison. *Ecology of Western Forests*. New York: Houghton Mifflin, 1993.

Grayson, Donald K. *The Desert's Past: A Natural Prehistory of the Great Basin*. Washington, D.C.: Smithsonian Institution, 1993.

Grubbs, Bruce. *Hiking Nevada*. Helena, Montana: Falcon Publishing, 1994.

Harmon, Will. *Wild Country Companion*. Helena, Montana: Falcon Publishing, 1994.

Hart, John. *Hiking the Great Basin: The High Desert Country of California, Nevada, Oregon, and Utah*. San Francisco: Sierra Club Books, 1991.

Houk, Rose. *Trails to Explore in Great Basin National Park*. Baker, Nevada: Great Basin Natural History Association, 1989.

Lambert, Darwin. *Great Basin Drama*. Niwot, Colorado: Roberts Rinehart Publishers, 1991.

National Park Service. *Final General Management Plan: Great Basin National Park*. Washington, D.C.: Department of the Interior, National Park Service, 1992.

Perry, John, and Jane Perry. *Sierra Club Guide to the Natural Areas of Oregon and Washington*. San Francisco: Sierra Club Books, 1983.

Preston, Gilbert. *Wilderness First Aid*. Helena, Montana: Falcon Publishing, 1997.

Schmidt, Jeremy. *Lehman Cave*. Baker, Nevada: Great Basin Natural History Association, 1987.

Trimble, Stephen. *Sagebrush Ocean: A Natural History of the Great Basin*. Reno, Nev.: University of Nevada Press, 1989.

Unrau, Harlan D. *A History of Great Basin National Park*. Washington, D.C.: Department of the Interior, National Park Service, 1990.

Wilkerson, James A. *Medicine for Mountaineering*. Seattle: The Mountaineers, 1992.

Wuerthner, George. *Nevada Mountain Ranges*. Helena, Montana: American and World Geographic Publishing, 1992.

Appendix C—Hiker's Checklist

This checklist may be keep you from forgetting anything essential. Of course, it contains far more items than are needed on any individual hiking trip.

Clothing
- [ ] shirt
- [ ] pants
- [ ] extra underwear
- [ ] swimsuit
- [ ] walking shorts
- [ ] belt or suspenders
- [ ] wind shell
- [ ] jacket or parka
- [ ] raingear
- [ ] gloves or mittens
- [ ] sun hat
- [ ] watch cap or balaclava
- [ ] sweater
- [ ] bandana

Footwear
- [ ] boots
- [ ] extra socks
- [ ] boot wax
- [ ] camp shoes

Sleeping Gear
- [ ] tarp or tent with fly
- [ ] groundsheet
- [ ] sleeping pad
- [ ] sleeping bag

Packs
- [ ] backpack
- [ ] day pack
- [ ] fanny pack

Cooking
- [ ] matches or lighter
- [ ] waterproof match case
- [ ] fire starter
- [ ] stove
- [ ] fuel
- [ ] stove maintenance kit
- [ ] cooking pot(s)
- [ ] cup
- [ ] bowl or plate

- [ ] utensils
- [ ] pot scrubber
- [ ] plastic water bottles with water
- [ ] collapsible water containers

Food

- [ ] cereal
- [ ] bread
- [ ] crackers
- [ ] cheese
- [ ] margarine
- [ ] dry soup
- [ ] packaged dinners
- [ ] snacks
- [ ] hot chocolate
- [ ] tea
- [ ] powdered milk
- [ ] powdered drink mixes

Navigation

- [ ] maps
- [ ] compass
- [ ] GPS receiver

Emergency/Repair

- [ ] pocket knife
- [ ] first aid kit
- [ ] snakebite kit
- [ ] nylon cord
- [ ] plastic bags
- [ ] wallet or ID card
- [ ] coins for phone calls
- [ ] pace blanket
- [ ] emergency fishing gear
      (hooks and a few feet of line)
- [ ] signal mirror
- [ ] pack parts
- [ ] stove parts
- [ ] tent parts
- [ ] flashlight bulbs, batteries
- [ ] scissors
- [ ] safety pins

Miscellaneous	☐ fishing gear
	☐ photographic gear
	☐ sunglasses
	☐ flashlight
	☐ candle lantern
	☐ sunscreen
	☐ insect repellent
	☐ toilet paper
	☐ trowel
	☐ binoculars
	☐ trash bags
	☐ notebook and pencils
	☐ field guides
	☐ book or game
	☐ dental and personal items
	☐ towel
	☐ water purification tablets or water filter
	☐ car key
	☐ watch
	☐ calendar
In Car	☐ extra water
	☐ extra food
	☐ extra clothes

About the Author

Bruce Grubbs has been hiking, cross-country skiing, and climbing in the Southwest for more than twenty-five years. He has participated in several technical first ascents of peaks in the Grand Canyon, as well as numerous long backpack trips. He has explored most of Arizona's wilderness areas, plus many places that are not yet officially protected. Bruce is the author of four other FalconGuides—*Hiking Oregon's Three Sisters Country*, *Hiking Northern Arizona*, *The Hiker's Guide to Nevada*, and *Hiking Arizona* (with Stewart Aitchison). He has also been a wildland firefighter and a partner in an outdoor shop. At present, he is a charter pilot and computer consultant, as well as a writer and photographer, and is based in Flagstaff, Arizona.

Index